THE A B C OF
STOCK SPECULATION

THE A B C OF
STOCK SPECULATION

BY

S. A. NELSON

Marketplace Books
Columbia, Maryland

THIS BOOK, ALONG WITH OTHER BOOKS, IS AVAILABLE AT DISCOUNTS THAT MAKE
IT REALISTIC TO PROVIDE THEM AS GIFTS TO YOUR CUSTOMERS, CLIENTS, AND STAFF.
FOR MORE INFORMATION ON THESE LONG LASTING, COST EFFECTIVE PREMIUMS,
PLEASE CALL US AT (800) 272-2855 OR YOU MAY EMAIL US AT SALES@TRADERSLIBRARY.
COM.

ISBN 1-59280-263-X
ISBN 978-1-59280-263-0

PRINTED IN THE UNITED STATES OF AMERICA.
1 2 3 4 5 6 7 8 9 0

PREFACE

Following the publication of The A B C of Wall Street there were many requests for a book dealing with the principles governing stock speculation. If there is one man better qualified than another to produce such a book that man is Mr. Charles H. Dow. Several attempts were made to have him write the desired volume but they were unavailing. From time to time in his Wall Street career, extending over a quarter of a century, Mr. Dow has carefully evolved his theories of successful stock speculation. They are to be found in Chapters IV to XX, inclusive, and can be commended to any one interested in stock speculation as remarkable for their grasp of a subject about which so little has been written and so much misinformation is gratuitously offered the public. In the preparation of this little volume thanks are also due to the Wall Street Journal, the Evening Post, the Dow, Jones & Co.'s News Agency, Mr. Alexander Dana Noyes, Mr. Daniel Kellogg, Mr. E. W. Harden, and a number of brokers and speculators. The reader of course understands that there is no royal road to success in speculation. It would be fallacy to undertake to show how money can be made. No infallible plan has yet been discovered. Experience and observation when intelligent, however, are valuable, and we are of the opinion that the average speculator will find a study of the following pages to be useful and profitable.

CONTENTS
THE A B C OF STOCK SPECULATION

From the Publisher
(2007 Edition)

Nelson's A B C of Stock Speculation may well be the grand daddy of all modern trading books. It was written during one of America's more fruitful decades, before the guns at Flanders pounded 19th century idealism into the dirt. In 1903, our government bank coffers were full to the brim and industrial output at record levels. It was the dawn of the new century and the upper middle class worker could buy a new car for $700 and a house from Sears and Roebuck and still have some cash left over for investments into a future prosperity.

These periods of abundance bred their own type of philosophers, many of whom were simply reacting to the growth and change fermenting around them. For S.A. Nelson, that voice from the Wall Street wilderness was Charles Dow, originator of the Dow Industrial Average. Nelson, a reporter for the Wall Street Journal, worked closely with Dow and, under his mentorship, he embraced the powerful message Dow spun into his columns and discussions. Dow, it seems, was far from an evangelizer. He simply saw things differently—possibly never realizing, at least openly, that he was propelling a new theory of stock speculation Nelson, like any great reporter, sensed the man and his times. He captured 15 chapters of Dow theory, placed them firmly into this landmark book, and cemented both of their names into economic history.

So what was it about Dow's insights that caught the attention of Nelson? Industrial output and the full mechanism of the transportation system had reached a point at which business could be viewed a a collective mass. We had moved beyond analyzing individual stocks and singular industries such as just railroads or steel. The market had reached a point whereby the trend could be calculated and with at least some degree of accuracy, it could be seen as either rising or falling in predictable patterns. Dow viewed more than just a company's output, he saw the general tide of business activity and the mass psychology behind movements.

This was powerful stuff in 1903! Nelson's book captures, in its very infancy, the trading psychology that would help guide generations of traders in speculative stocks. It would be the subtle impetus of countless charting systems and theories on trading psychology. But Nelson's book is more than Dow's introduction onto the stage of trading immortality, it gives credence to an occupation that has always walked the fine line of five-card draw. As Nelson says, "Speculation is a venture based on calculation. Gambling is a venture without calculation. The law makes the distinction: it sustains speculation, and condemns gambling."

Nelson also paints a full panorama of the stock market roller coaster ride, complete with all its colorful theatrics. He talks of the "tipsters" and the "hucksters," the "Bucket Shops," and the ever passionate topic of stock manipulation. He gives the reader the facts. He tells us to stay true to our course and gives us ample examples of foolish panic. "Men rather than markets differ," he says. By this he means that the fundamentals of good business remain consistent while men fight in trenches and riot against aristocracy. Read this book and you'll have a better understanding of the complexity of your task, the scope of your profession, and the shoulders that it takes to survive…and win.

CHAPTER I.

Origin of Stock Brokers, Stock Exchanges and Stock Speculation.

Etymological authorities are not in entire accord respecting the origin of the word "Broker." Jacob's Law Dictionary says: "The etymology of the term Broker has been variously given. By some it has been derived from the Saxon *broc,* misfortune, as denoting a broken trader; the occupation being formerly confined, it is said, to unfortunate persons of that description (Tomlins). According to others it was formed from the French *broieur,* a grinder or breaker into small pieces; a Broker being one who *beats* or draws a bargain into particulars (Termes de la Ley, Cowell). The law Latin from *obrocator,* however, seems to point distinctly to the Saxon *abroecan* (to break), as the true root, which in the old word *abbrochment* (q. v.) or *abroachment,* had the sense of breaking up goods or selling at retail. A Broker, therefore, would seem to have been originally a *retailer,* and hence we find the old word *auctionarius* (q. v.) used in both these senses (Barrill's Law Diet., tit. "Broker"). Wharton gives, as the derivation of the word the French *broceur,* and the Latin *tritor,* a person who breaks into small pieces (Whar. Law Diet., tit. "Broker"). Webster gives as its derivation, the old English *brocour,* Norman French *broggour,* French *brocanteur.* Under the word "broke," to deal in second hand goods, to be a Broker, Webster says it is probably derived from the word *brock.* Worcester derives it from the Anglo-Saxon *brucan,* to discharge an office; *brocian,* to oppress; and the French *broyer,* to grind. See "Broke" and "Broker." The word "Broker" seems first to occur in literature in Pier's Ploughman, "Among

1

burgeises have I be Dwellyng at London. And gart Backbiting be a brocour. To blame men's ware." It clearly means here a *fault find-er,* as in Provencal *brac* is refuse. The Broker was originally one who inspected goods and rejected what was below the standard (Wedgwood). Crabb's Dig. of Stat., tit. "Brokers," 261, says, "There were a class of persons known to the Romans who were deemed public officers, and who united the functions of bankers, exchangers, Brokers, commissioners and notaries all in one under the description of *proxe netae.*"

As early as 1285, in England, the term Broker occurs in an Act of Parliament. It enacts that "there shall be no Broker in the city (London), except those who are admitted and sworn before the warden, mayor or aldermen."

John E. Dos Passos, an authority on stock exchange law, says: "The next statute passed in the reign of James the First, more than 300 years later (1604) regulates the calling of Brokers with greater detail than the first act and clearly shows, by the use of the words 'merchandise and wares' that down to this period the Broker in money, stock, and funds had no legal existence. . . It was not until the latter part of the seventeenth century, when the East India Company came prominently before the public, that trading or speculating in stock became an established business in England; and the term 'Broker,' which had then a well-understood meaning was promptly transferred to those persons who were employed to buy or sell stocks or shares, and who thenceforth became known as 'stock-brokers.'"

In 1697 owing to the "unjust practices and designs" of Brokers and Stock-jobbers in selling tallies, bank stock, bank bills, shares and interest in joint stock, a stringent act was passed permitting only sworn appointees to act as Brokers. In the reigns of William III., Anne and George, statutes were passed regulating the practice and trade of Brokers.

An early legal writer describing Stockbrokers said: "Stockbrokers are persons who confine their transactions to the buying and selling of property in the public funds and other securities for money, and they are employed by the proprietors or holders of the said securities. Of late years, owing to the prodigious increase of the funded debt of the nation, commonly called the stock, they are becoming a very numerous and considerable body, and have built by subscription, a room near the Bank, wherein they meet to transact business with their principals, and with each other; and to prepare and settle their proceedings before they go to the transfer-offices at the Bank, the South Sea and India houses, thereby preventing a great deal of confusion at the public offices, where the concourse of people is so great during the hours of transferring stock that if the business was not prepared beforehand it would be impossible to transact it within the given time." The advantage of having a Broker as an intermediary was recognized by merchants many centuries ago. A sixteenth century writer on the law says: "It is an old proverb, and very true, that between *what you will buy?* and *what you will sell?* There are twenty in the hundred differing in the price, which is the cause that all the nations do more effect to sell their commodities with reputation by means of Brokers than we do; for that which seems to be gotten thereby is more than double lost another way. Besides, that by that course many differences are prevented which arise between man and man in their bargains or verbal contracts; for the testimony of a sworn Broker and his book together is sufficient to end the same."

Dealings in Stock certificates constitute the main business of Stock-brokers, but the origin of stock certificates has not been satisfactorily traced beyond the middle of the seventeenth century. Property in this form was not known to the ancient law. While mercantile or commercial corporations existed among the

Romans, history gives us no information regarding their character or methods of conduct.

Ang. & Ames on Corporations (10th ed.) Ch. 18, Sec. 26, says: "A *Collegium Mercatorum* existed at Rome 493 B. C. but the modern bourse from the Latin *bursa,* a purse, originated about the fifteenth century. Bourges and Amsterdam contend for the honor of having erected the first bourse."

"The Roman law," says John R. Dos Passos, "required three persons to organize a corporation; and as each body had at least that number of members, if not more, it would seem but natural that a certificate, or some other substantial muniment of title, should have been issued by the corporation to its respective members, in which the proportion of interest of each in the capital or corporate property of the association appeared. But whether a certificate was, in fact, issued, and, if so, was regarded as property capable of sale or other negotiation, and of vesting in the representatives of the owner, on his decease, or whether the corporations were all of the nature of guilds conferring upon the members mere *personal* rights—all of these questions seem now to be incapable of solution; and the Roman law, which sheds such floods of light upon commercial subjects apparently leaves the above matters in total darkness."

In England, in 1770, Lord Mansfield in a case wherein it was contended that stock certificates were *money* decided against that view, saying: "This is a *new* species of property *arisen within the compass of a few years.* It is not money."

The Stock Exchange or Bourse in its present use is a modern creation. Brokers and dealers in stocks and merchandise dealt together in an exchange in Cornhill, London, in 1670, or thereabouts. In 1698, the Stock-brokers of London obtained quarters for their exclusive use.

The first Stock Exchange formed in the United States was that of Philadelphia, where a Board of Stock-brokers formally organized and adopted a constitution in the early part of the eighteenth century.

The New York Stock Exchange, framed on the plan of the one in Philadelphia, was organized in 1817, but curiously enough this institution is in possession of a document hearing dated May 17, 1792, signed by a number of Brokers, in which it is stated: "We, the subscribers, Brokers for the purchase and sale of public business, agree to do business at not less than one-fourth of one per cent."

Medberry, in his "Men and Mysteries of Wall Street," describes early stock speculation in this country as follows: "When Washington was President, and Continental money was worth a trifle more as currency than as waste paper, some twenty New York dealers in public stock met together in a Broker's office and signed their names in the bold, strong hand of their generation, to an agreement of the nature of a protective league. The date of this paper is May 17, 1792. The volume of business of all these primitive New York Brokers could not have been much above that of even the poorest first-class Wall Street house in our time (1870). The Revolutionary shinplasters, as the irreverent already styled them, were spread over the land in such plenty that there were $100 to each inhabitant. Something was to be made, therefore, from the fluctuations to which they were liable. Indeed, one of the greatest Broker firms of subsequent years derived its capital from the lucky speculations of its senior member in this currency.

"The war of 1812 gave the first genuine impulse to stock speculation. The Government issued sixteen million in Treasury notes, and put loans amounting to one hundred and nine million on the market. There were endless fluctuations and the lazy-going capitalists of the time managed to gain or lose handsome fortunes. Bank stock was also a favorite investment. An illustration of one of the sources of money-making to Brokers at this period is found in the fact that United States 6s of 1814 were at 50 in specie and 70 in New York bank currency.

"In 1816 one could count up two hundred banks with a capital of $82,000,000. . . . One day in 1817, the New York stock dealers met in the room of an associate and voted to send a 'delegate' over on the stage line to investigate the system adopted in the rival city (Philadelphia). The Philadelphia visit was successful; and the draft of a constitution and by-laws, framed from that of the Philadelphia Board, received the final approbation of a sufficient number of Brokers to enable the New York Stock Exchange to become a definite fact. Three years after, on the 21st of February, 1820, this preliminary code of rules received a thorough revision and the organization was strengthened by the accession of some of the heaviest capitalists in the city. Indeed, with 1820, the real history of the Exchange may properly be said to commence."

In Europe stock speculation historically was marked with white stones by the "Tulip Craze," the South Sea Bubble, the John Law inflation in France, and later by the wild speculation in Kaffirs.

In this country for more than half a century stock speculation had its basis in the securities of the steam railroad. It has ebbed and flowed with the promotion, construction, decline, and reorganization of that industry.

In the last decade speculation has been fostered by the "industrial proposition," which has resulted in offering to the public shares of industrial corporations. Not an industry has been passed by. Like the railroad the industrial corporation is destined to have its periods of promotion, construction, decline and reorganization. It will not be difficult for the reader to determine which period he has under immediate consideration.

CHAPTER II.

Stock Speculation.

For many years stock speculation has been of national and absorbing importance. During the period from 1896 to 1902 investment and speculation in corporate securities attained an unprecedented importance, owing to the general movement to combine and incorporate industrial companies with a consequent change of ownership. Ownership which had been vested in small groups of individuals now became widely distributed. Where an industry had been controlled and owned by 10 persons the number multiplied and increased by 10 and 1,000-fold through the medium of share ownership. The mine and the factory owned by the individual were merged into a joint corporation, the shares of which were listed on the Stock Exchange, and offered to the public for investment or speculation. The United States Steel Corporation has more than 40,000 stockholders; the American Sugar Refining, 11,000; while other corporations, notably those representing the railroad, are relatively as widely distributed. Stock speculation in the United States in the period named was also inspired by the rehabilitation of the railroad industry, the stocks of which have always been favorite speculative fuel, and the basis for the intense public interest and activity was the general prosperity and wealth of the country. A variety of causes contributed to the tremendous increase in national wealth. To-day, speculation in the shares listed on the New York Stock Exchange is not only confined to New York but extends to California on the West, Canada on the North, Texas on the South and London, Paris and Berlin on the East.

The telegraph, telephone and cable wire transmits quotations to facilitate speculation to-day with a speed and perfection of method that would have been regarded as marvelous by the founders of the New York Stock Exchange, and quite impossible by the great manipulators who dominated the arena a quarter of a century ago. Millions of dollars are consumed annually in order to keep the machinery of Wall Street in working order. It is estimated that the annual expenses of 300 leading Wall Street stock firms approximate $15,000,000. In view of the commercial and economic tendencies of the times, the indications are that stock speculation will continue to play a highly important part in the country's trade. In 1901 there were days when dealings on the Stock Exchange exceeded 3,000,000 shares and the machinery of speculation threatened to break down under the intensity of the strain to which it was subjected. Whether the records of that year will ever be broken no man can foretell, but it is reasonable to say that not for a long time will interest in the daily changes of the stock market be confined solely to the ranks of the professional stock speculator who conducts his operations within stone's throw of the Stock Exchange, for there has arisen a vast army of investors and speculators who are deeply interested in the day's price fluctuations.

CHAPTER III.

STOCK SPECULATION AND GAMBLING.

Is there any difference between speculation and gambling? The terms are often used interchangeably, but speculation pre-supposes intellectual effort; gambling blind chance. Accurately to define the two is difficult; all definitions are difficult. Wit and humor, for instance, can be defined; but notwithstanding the most subtle distinction, wit and humor blend, run into each other. This is true of speculation and gambling. The reform has some elements of chance; the latter some of the elements of reason. We define as best we can. Speculation is a venture based upon calculation. Gambling is a venture without calculation. The law makes this distinction: it sustains speculation, and condemns gambling. All business is more or less speculative. The term speculation, however, is commonly restricted to business of exceptional uncertainty. The uninitiated believe that chance is so large a part of speculation that it is subject to no rules, is governed by no laws. This is a serious error.—Unknown writer.

Is a broker a trader, a speculator or a manipulator a gambler? Or are all four gamblers? An old speculator takes this somewhat humorous view of the question: "I am not a gambler—the broker is the gambler—I am the lamb, unshorn it's true, but nevertheless the victim of a bad habit. If I enter a gambling house and make a few wagers I would resent the imputation that I was a gambler. I am not a gambler or at the worst only an amateur at the game and then for a few minutes only. The man who backs the game and runs the gambling house is the professional gambler. Now the broker occupies much the same relationship to the stock gambling game that the man with the cards and wheel does to his peculiar trade. Of course behind the stock broker there is the manipulator and the game itself. The broker does not lose out his own money unless he 'buckets' his orders (when he is a gambler as is every bucket shop operator) so he is only a 'croupier' so to speak, for the game. A stock speculator whose only source of income is stock speculation on a margin may fairly call himself a gambler."

Speculation and gambling, as the words are used to-day, are substantially interchangeable, but nevertheless there is a marked distinction between the two. All speculators are not necessarily gamblers, although all stock gamblers (traders) are speculators. When speculation in stocks becomes gambling in stocks, the operations are usually confined to transactions made on a margin.

For example: A walks in a broker's office and asks: "What do you think of the market?" "We hear," is the reply, "that St. Paul is a purchase at the opening for a rise of several points." "Very well, buy me 100 shares, sell at 2 points profit and stop the loss at 1 point." Obviously this is a wager in which the gambling factor is very strong and the maker regards himself as a gambler.

Example No. 2: B enters the same office, asks the same question, receives the same reply and says: "Very well, buy me 100 shares, send the certificate to my office and I will give you a check for it." B buys his stock outright and would not buy a single share on a margin. He will admit that he is a speculator, but will be insulted if you call him a gambler.

Example No. 3: C is a trader and an Exchange member. Ask him his business and he will reply that he is a trader. Ask him to define a trader and he will say: "As far as I am concerned a trader is a gambler. I never go home long or short a share of stock. I take advantage of the smallest changes in the market limiting my losses to the minimum—⅛ s and ¼ s—and take equally small profits, although I am glad to get larger ones. I excel at calling the successive changes, trade on either side, and have no pronounced views as to whether it is a bull or bear market."

All bucket shop operators and traders are gamblers.

Investors are not gamblers.

Brokers and manipulators are not necessarily gamblers, the circumstances governing individual cases.

The case of B will doubtless cause discussion, but his view is that he is no more a gambler than the man who buys a parcel of real estate on a 10 per cent equity or the merchant who buys and sells goods in expectation of a rise or fall.

But stock speculation does not owe its importance to the classes of speculators enumerated as closely allied to the gambler. On the contrary they are in the minority. Gambling may at times be an unavoidable accompaniment of stock speculation, but stock speculation is so interwoven with the money market and the commerce of the country that to eliminate it from the world of business would be for civilization to take a long backward step.

Criticism of stock speculation as of other trades, arts and sciences, to be intelligent, should be discriminating. Pulpit and press at times denounce stock speculation as if the Stock Exchange and Wall Street were hotbeds of corruption.

No well-informed man questions the usefulness of the Stock Exchange or stock speculator. Stock Exchange prices register values and the state of trade, precisely as a thermometer registers heat or cold. The stock market is the most highly organized and delicately adjusted market in the world. It offers to the public large securities which are good collaterals at any bank and securities which on any business day can be sold for cash. It gives the money market great elasticity. It is a safeguard provided for unexpected demands upon the money market, and furnishes a medium of exchange that minimizes the use of gold in international operations. It is a most important part of the modern system of credit. Eliminate the stock market and transferable securities from the life of the country to-day and contemplate if good can be the result of a demand from Europe for its credit balances to be paid in gold. The result would paralyze industrial progress. The Stock Exchange facilitates the employment of capital, adds to its productiveness, is an accurately registering machinery of credit indispensable to the banks of the country, and is a guiding force for the merchant and financier.

CHAPTER IV.

THE MORALITY OF WALL STREET.

A leading newspaper commented (1902) editorially on the morality of Wall Street. Part of the burden of its comment was that it was different in some respects from morality elsewhere. Taking the word "morality" to mean in this instance the general law or code of ethics obtaining in Wall Street and elsewhere, it does not appear that there is any essential difference between Wall Street morality and general business morality.

The object of all business is the "making of money" and nothing else. Wall Street is certainly no different from any other place or center of business activity in this respect. Where one business center or group of industries differs from another in the matter of morality is probably only in the details of its code. Now, in the details of its code Wall Street will compare to advantage with most other business centers. As has been pointed out, its machinery is predicated upon rigid observance of bargains made and word passed. While it is true that this kind of honor is absolutely necessary for the smooth conduct of business as it is carried on in Wall Street, it is also true that the high standard required is lived up to by the Street, and breaches thereof are extremely rare.

Perhaps one reason why there is so much disposition to question the morality of Wall Street and contrast it unfavorably with the morality of other business centers is the fact that in Wall Street probably to a greater extent than elsewhere the primal passions and instincts of acquisitiveness and self-preservation wear less disguise than they do in the other channels of industry and money making. A Stock Exchange anywhere is a theatre in which these primal passions battle as gladiators in the arena without concealment or pretense. Every one who goes down into the arena knows that it is a battle wherein his hand must keep his head, and the penalty of failure will be exacted against him to the utmost. *"A la guerre comma a la guerre"* is a proverb that very well describes the conditions under which business is done in Wall Street. Elsewhere it may appear to be different. The only difference is that in Wall Street there is no pretense, no disguise; the essential struggle is the same everywhere. In Wall Street, there has been and unfortunately still is at times fraud in detail peculiar to Wall Street, but it is not of Wall Street nor inherent in the laws of the game.

It is true that speculation in Wall Street is looked upon as being especially immoral by comparison with speculation elsewhere. It is, however, part of almost every manufacturer's business or of every merchant's business to speculate in raw materials or goods, and nobody thinks of finding fault with either for doing so. In Wall Street speculation stands alone, without any business disguise, for all men to see. There is no difference between one kind of speculation and another so far as essence is concerned; the only difference is that one is disguised and the other is not. It may be noted, moreover, that where the speculation is not disguised it is apt to be more honest than where it hides under a cloak of business enterprise. All men are gamblers and always will be more or less for the "get rich quick" idea, and the chances of "something for nothing" will always prove irresistibly attractive to human nature.

The plain fact of the matter is that the general suspicion of and hostility toward Wall Street find their root in the fact that the race for money is carried on simply, openly in the light of day, without pretense or hypocrisy of any kind, and without attempt to cloak the passions that have existed since man first came upon the earth. If gambling be wrong, the principal charge that can be levied against Wall Street is that it is there carried on openly, under simple but rigid rules, and Wall Street does not care who knows it. Elsewhere it goes on in essence just the same, but disguised in a multitude of ways. In these days most forms of business must of their very nature contain a large element of speculation. We do not see that speculation becomes more immoral by being openly carried on.

Wall Street has rather less use for a habitual liar than have other places. It has no use at all for a man who does not keep his word. It may be true that honesty is the best policy in Wall Street, simply for reasons of convenience, but that it is the best policy no one can deny. In fact, it is the only policy that in the long run is successful. We do not think that this is necessarily an argument against the morality of Wall Street.

CHAPTER V.

[1]SCIENTIFIC SPECULATION.

T he question whether there is such a thing as scientific speculation is often asked. Various answers of a somewhat affirmative character have been given but they have generally been hedged about with so many qualifications as to be nearly useless for practical purposes. The experiences of operators have, however, crystallized into some general rules worth heeding.

The maxim "buy cheap and sell dear" is as old as speculation itself, but it leaves unsolved the question of when a security of a commodity is cheap and when it is dear, and this is the vital point.

The elder Rothschilds are said to have acted on the principle that it was well to buy a property of known value when others wanted to sell and to sell when others wanted to buy. There is a great deal of sound wisdom in this. The public, as a whole, buys at the wrong time and sells at the wrong time. The reason is that markets are made in part by manipulation and the public buys on manipulated advances and after they are well along. Hence it buys at the time when manipulators wish to sell and sells when manipulators wish to buy.

In some commission offices, there are traders who, as a rule, go against whatever the outside customers of the house are doing. When members of the firm say, "all our customers are getting long of stocks," these traders sell out; but they buy when the firm says, "the customers are all short." There are of course, exceptions

---

[1] Dow's Theory.

to this rule. If there were no exceptions, the keepers of bucket shops would all get rich. When the market has an extraordinary rise, the public makes money, in spite of beginning its purchases at what would ordinarily be the wrong time, and this is when the bucket shops either lose their money or close out in order to keep such money of customers as they have in hand.

All of this points to the soundness of the Rothschild principle of buying a property of known value when the public generally is disposed to sell; or of selling it when the general public thinks it a time to buy.

Daniel Drew used to say, "cut your losses short, but let your profits run." This was good preaching, but "Uncle Dan" did not, in his later years, practice his rule, when it would have been better for him if he had. The thought here is unquestionably one of the sound principles in trading. It means that if a stock has been purchased and it goes up, it is well to wait; but if it goes down, it is well to stop the loss quickly on the ground that the theory on which the purchase was made was wrong.

The public, as a whole, exactly reverses this rule. The average operator, when he sees two or three points profit, takes it; but, if a stock goes against him two or three points, he holds on waiting for the price to recover, with, oftentimes, the result of seeing a loss of two or three points run into a loss of ten points. He then becomes discouraged and sells out near the bottom to protect the margin in which he has left.

How many operators in looking over their books find a considerable number of small profits swept away by one large loss? When a trader finds by his accounts that his profits have been relatively large and his losses relatively small, he can make up his mind that he is learning how to trade.

The trouble with carrying out this plan is that a series of losses of from 1½ to 2 points are very discouraging. A trader who sees that he has taken twice or three times a loss of two points when, if he had waited a few days he need not have taken any loss, is very apt to decide that he will not cut his losses short any more, but will wait, and this is the time when the recovery does not come.

Mr. Jay Gould said his policy was to endeavor to foresee future conditions in a property and then, having made his commitments carefully, to exercise great patience in awaiting results. This also is sound doctrine, but proceeds along very different lines. Assuming the ability to foresee the future, it is the wisest of all courses; but many who have tried this method have found that the omission of essential factors made their forecast valueless, and both their courage and their patience of little avail. Nevertheless, this method should not be discarded on account of the difficulties involved. Within limitations, the future can be foreseen. The present is always tending toward the future and there are always in existing conditions signals of danger or encouragement for those who read with care.

CHAPTER VI.

[1] THE TWO GENERAL METHODS OF TRADING.

There are two general methods of trading. One is to deal in active stocks in comparatively large amounts, relying for protection upon stop orders. In this method of trading it is not necessary to know much about the values. The point of chief importance is that the stock should be active enough to permit the execution of the stop order at the point selected so as to cut losses short. The operator, by this method, guesses which way the stock will move. If he guesses right, he lets his profits run. If he guesses wrong, he goes out on the stop order. If he can guess right as often as he can guess wrong, he is fairly sure of profits.

The other system is an entirely different proposition. It starts with the assumption that the operator knows approximately the value of the stock in which he proposes to deal. It assumes that he has considered the tendency of the general market; that he realizes whether the stock in which he proposes to deal is relatively up or down, and that he feels sure of its value for at least months to come.

Suppose this to exist: The operator lays out his plan of campaign on the theory that he will buy his first lot of stock at what he considers the right price and the right time and will then buy an equal amount every 1 per cent down as far as the decline may go.

---

[1]   Dow's Theory.

This method of trading is the one generally employed by large operators. They know the value of the stock in which they propose to deal, and are therefore reasonably secure in following a decline. They feel about a stock as merchants feel about buying staple goods. If an article is cheap at $100, they know it is cheaper at $90 and will strain a point to buy at $80 or at $70, knowing that the price must recover. This is the way a large operator looks at his favorite stocks and this is why he generally makes money in them.

The disadvantage of the small operator in following this method is two-fold. He does not absolutely know the value of the stock. That is, he may know the truth up to a certain point, but beyond that is an unknown factor which interferes with the result. When the price of a stock declines considerably, the small operator always fears that he has overlooked something of importance, and he is therefore tempted to sell instead of averaging his holdings.

The second disadvantage of the small operator in following this policy is that he seldom provides sufficient capital for his requirements. Thousands of speculators believe that because 10 per cent is a common speculative margin, that $1,000 justifies them in trading in hundred share lots. This impression produces losses continually.

The man who has $1,000 for speculation is not well equipped for trading in even 10 share lots, if he proposes to deal on a scale. A comparison of high and low prices of active stocks shows frequently a difference of 30 points in a year. Any operator proposing to follow a stock down, buying on a scale, should make his preparations for a possible fall of from 20 to 30 points. Assuming that he does not begin to buy until his stock is 5 points down from the top, there is still a possibility of having to buy 20 lots before the turn will come.

If, however, an outsider will provide $2,500 as his specu-lative capital and will trade in ten-share lots in a thoroughly good railroad stock, beginning his purchases only after a decline of five points in a rising market, and ten points in a bear market, following the decline with purchases every point down, and retaining all the stock bought, he seldom need make a loss.

Such campaigns require time, patience, and the pursuance of a fixed policy, but whoever will follow this policy will find himself able to get a high rate of interest on the capital invested. It is an old saying in Wall Street that the man who begins to speculate in stocks with the intention of making a fortune, usually goes broke, whereas the man who trades with a view of getting good interest on his money, sometimes gets rich.

This is only another way of saying that money is made by conservative trading rather than by the effort to get large profits by taking large risks. After allowing for all the risks involved, we think the outsider who wants to trade in stocks has a better chance working in small lots on a scale than in any other way, provided he will pay attention to certain essential points, which for convenience of reference we will enumerate in order.

1. Bull markets and bear markets run four and five years at a time. Determine by the average prices, which one is under way.
2. Determine the stock or stocks to trade in. They should be railroad stocks, dividend payers, not too low, nor too high, fairly active, and for the bull side below their value; for the bear side above their value. Values are determined roughly by the earnings available for dividends.
3. Observe the position of your stock with relation to recent fluctuations. In a bull market, the time to begin to buy is when a stock has had four or five

points decline from the last previous top. In a bear market, the time to begin to sell is when such a stock has had three or four points rally from the bottom.

4. Stick to the stock bought until a fair profit or until there is good reason for deciding that the first estimate of value was wrong. Remember that an active stock will generally rally from ⅜ per cent to ⅝ per cent of the amount of its decline under adverse conditions and more than that under favorable conditions.

5. Have money enough to see a decline through without becoming uneasy or over-burdened. $2,500 ought to take care of a ten-share scale every point down—that is to say, supposing the first lot to be bought five points down from the top, $2,500 ought to carry the scale until the natural recovery from the low point brings the lot out with a profit on the average cost. It will not do to expect a profit on every lot, but only on the average. In a bull market it is better to always work on the bull side; in a bear market, on the bear side. There are usually more rallies in a bear market than there are relapses in a bull market.

6. Do not let success in making money in ten-share lots create a belief that a bolder policy will be wiser and begin to trade in 100-share lots with inadequate capital. A few hundred-share losses will wipe out a good many ten-share profits.

7. There is not usually much difficulty in dealing in ten-share lots on the short side. If one broker does not wish to do it, another probably will, especially for a customer who amply protects his account and who seems to understand what he is doing.

CHAPTER VII.

[1]THREE GENERAL LINES OF REASONING.

We have spoken in a preceding article of the fact that the experience of great interests in the market seems to have crystallized into three general lines of reasoning.

The first is that the surface appearance of the market is apt to be deceptive. The second is that it is well in trading to cut losses short and let profits run. The third is that correctly discounting the future is a sure and easy road to wealth. The problem is how these rules which are undoubtedly sound can be operated in a practical way.

Let us take first the action of the general market with reference to the time to buy. The market is always to be considered as having three movements, all going on at the same time. The first is the narrow movement from day to day. The second is the short swing, running from two weeks to a month or more; the third is the main movement covering at least four years in its duration.

The day to day movement should be disregarded by everybody, except traders, who pay no commissions. The medium swing is the one for ordinary consideration. The outside trader should not attempt to deal in more than two or three stocks at a time. He should keep a chart of the price movements of these stocks so as to know their swings for months or years, and thus be able to tell readily where in the general swing his particular stocks appear to be.

---

[1]   Dow's Theory.

He should keep with his price movement a record of the volume of transactions and notes of any special facts hearing on that property, such as increases or decreases in earnings, increases in fixed charges, development of floating debt, and above all the actual dividend earnings as shown from month to month. He should observe the movement of the general market as indicated by the averages published daily,[2] as this shows the market more clearly than it is shown by any one stock.

The main purpose of this study is to enable the trader to determine, first, the value of the stock he is in—whether it is increasing or decreasing—and, second, when the time to buy seems opportune. Assuming the thirty day swing to be about 5 points, it is in the highest degree desirable not to buy when three of these points have passed, as such a purchase limits the probable profits to about two points.

It is therefore generally wise to look for a low point on a decline. Suppose, for instance, that Union Pacific was the stock under consideration; that it was clearly selling below its value, and that a bull market for the four-year period was under way. Assuming further that in a period of reaction Union Pacific had fallen four points from the previous highest. Assume earnings and prospects to be favorable and the outlook for the general market to be about normal.

This would be the time to begin to buy Union Pacific. The prudent trader, however, would take only part of his line. He would buy perhaps one-half of the stock he wanted and then give an order to buy the remainder as the price declined. The fall might go much further than he anticipated. It might be necessary to wait a long time for profit. There might even be developments which would make it wise to throw over the stock bought with the hope of replacing it materially lower.

---

[2]   See Wall Street Journal.

These, however, are all exceptions. In a majority of cases this method of choosing the time to buy, founded upon clear perception of value in the stock chosen and close observation of the market swings under way will enable an operator to secure stock at a time and at a price which will give fair profits on the investment.

CHAPTER VIII.

[1]SWINGS WITHIN SWINGS.

A correspondent asks: "For some time you have been writing rather bullish on the immediate market, yet a little bearish in a larger sense. How do you make this consistent?"

We get this question in one form or another rather frequently. It denotes a lack of familiarity with fluctuations in prices when viewed over considerable periods. Many people seem to think that the change in prices in any one day is complete in itself and bears no relation to larger movements which may be under way. This is not so.

Nothing is more certain than that the market has three well defined movements which fit into each other. The first is the daily variation due to local causes and the balance of buying or selling at that particular time. The secondary movement covers a period ranging from ten days to sixty days, averaging probably between thirty and forty days. The third move is the great swing covering from four to six years.

In thinking about the market, it is necessary to think with reference to each of these periods in order to take advantage of opportunities. If the main move is up, relapses are speculators' opportunities, but if the main move is down, rallies furnish these opportunities.

Losses should not generally be taken on the long side in a bull period. Nor should they generally be taken on the short

---

[1] Dow's Theory.

side in a bear period. It is a bull period as long as the average of one high point exceeds that of previous high points. It is a bear period when the low point becomes lower than the previous low points. It is often difficult to judge whether the end of an advance has come because the movement of prices is that which would occur if the main tendency had changed. Yet, it may only be an unusually pronounced secondary movement.

The first thing for any operator to consider is the value of the stock in which he proposes to trade. The second is to determine the direction of the main movement of prices. We know of nothing more instructive on this point than the course of prices as printed daily.[2] The third thing is to determine the position of the secondary swing.

Assume for instance that the stock selected was Union Pacific; that the course of prices afforded clear evidence of a bull market under way; that the high point in Union Pacific thirty days ago was 108; that the price had slowly declined in sympathy with the market and without special new features to 98. The chances would be in favor of buying a part of the line wanted at that price with the intention of buying a little more if the stock had further decline or if the price showed a well defined advancing tendency. It would then be wise to watch the general market and wait for an advance.

A 10-point decline under such conditions would be almost certain to bring in a bull market more than 5 points recovery and full 10 points would not be unreasonable; hence if the general market maintained a good tone, it would be wise to wait for 5 points and then begin to think about stop orders.

Even in a bear market, this method of trading will usually be found safe, although the profit taken should be less because

---

[2]   See Wall Street Journal.

of the liability of weak spots breaking out and checking the general rise.

CHAPTER IX.

[1]METHODS OF READING THE MARKET.

A correspondent writes: "Is there any way of forecasting the course of the market from the tape, from
your records of transactions or from the summarized
movement of prices? Transactions must mean something, but
how can a trader tell what they mean?"

This is an old question. There have been a variety of answers
but it is doubtful if any have been or can be wholly satisfactory.
Several methods, however, are in practical use and at times afford
suggestions.

There is what is called the book method. Prices are set down,
giving each change of 1 point as it occurs, thereby forming lines
having a general horizontal direction but running into diagonals
as the market moves up and down. There come times when a
stock with a good degree of activity will stay within a narrow
range of prices, say 2 points, until there has formed quite a
long horizontal line of these figures. The formation of such a
line sometimes suggests that stock has been accumulated or
distributed, and this leads other people to buy or sell at the same
time. Records of this kind kept for the last fifteen years seem to
support the theory that the manipulation necessary to acquire
stock is often times detected in this way.

Another method is what is called the theory of double tops.
Records of trading show that in many cases when a stock reaches
top it will have a moderate decline and then go back again to

---

[1]   Dow's Theory.

near the highest figures. If after such a move, the price again recedes, it is liable to decline some distance.

Those, however, who attempt to trade on this theory alone find a good many exceptions and a good many times when signals are not given.

There are those who trade on the theory of averages. It is true that in a considerable period of time the market has about as many days of advance as it has of decline. If there come a series of days of advance, there will almost surely come the balancing days of decline.

The trouble with this system is that the small swings are always part of the larger swings, and while the tendency of events equally liable to happen is always toward equality, it is also true that every combination possible is liable to occur, and there frequently come long swings, or, in the case of stock trading, an extraordinary number of days of advance or decline which fit properly into the theory when regarded on a long scale, but which are calculated to upset any operations based on the expectation of a series of short swings.

A much more practicable theory is that founded on the law of action and reaction. It seems to be a fact that a primary movement in the market will generally have a secondary movement in the opposite direction of at least three-eighths of the primary movement. If a stock advances 10 points, it is very likely to have a relapse of 4 points or more. The law seems to hold good no matter how far the advance goes. A rise of 20 points will not infrequently bring a decline of 8 points or more. It is impossible to tell in advance the length of any primary movement, but the further it goes, the greater the reaction when it comes, hence the more certainty of being able to trade successfully on that reaction.

A method employed by some operators of large experience is that of responses. The theory involved is this: The market is always under more or less manipulation. A large operator who is seeking to advance the market does not buy everything on the list, but puts up two or three leading stocks either by legitimate buying or by manipulation. He then watches the effect on the other stocks. If sentiment is bullish, and people are disposed to take hold, those who see this rise in two or three stocks immediately begin to buy other stocks and the market rises to a higher level. This is the public response, and is an indication that the leading stocks will be given another lift and that the general market will follow.

If, however, leading stocks are advanced and others do not follow, it is evidence that the public is not disposed to buy. As soon as this is clear the attempt to advance prices is generally discontinued. This method is employed more particularly by those who watch the tape. But it can be read at the close of the day in our record of transactions by seeing what stocks were put up within specified hours and whether the general market followed or not. The best way of reading the market is to read from the standpoint of values. The market is not like a balloon plunging hither and thither in the wind. As a whole, it represents a serious, well considered effort on the part of far-sighted and well-informed men to adjust prices to such values as exist or which are expected to exist in the not too remote future. The thought with great operators is not whether a price can be advanced, but whether the value of property which they propose to buy will lead investors and speculators six months hence to take stock at figures from 10 to 20 points above present prices.

In reading the market, therefore, the main point is to discover what a stock can be expected to be worth three months hence and then to see whether manipulators or investors are advancing the price of that stock toward those figures. It is often possible to read movements in the market very clearly in this way. To know values is to comprehend the meaning of movements in the market.

CHAPTER X.

[1]THE OPERATION OF STOP ORDERS.

A correspondent inquires: "My brokers advise me to protect my transactions by stop orders. It seems to me that stop orders may be good for brokers by giving them commissions, but they make customers take unnecessary losses. Do you advise speculators to give stop orders?"

Proof on this point is afforded by taking a large number of fluctuations and seeing how the average works out. We believe that for the margin trader, and especially the trader who operates rather more largely than he ought on the margin that he has, stop orders are wise. There are, however, many qualifications which should be kept in mind.

If a man is trading as a semi-investor, using 50 per cent margin, depending on values for his profit and operating in harmony with the main tendency of the market, we do not think a stop order desirable. To explain this a little more fully: Suppose the movement of averages shows that the market is in a rising period, such periods usually covering several years with only temporary reversals in direction. Suppose that an operator finds that a certain stock is earning an abnormal percentage on its market value, or, in other words, is intrinsically cheap. Suppose on the occasion of a temporary setback this stock is bought to be carried for months if necessary until the price has risen to approximately the level of the value. A stop order is folly in a case of this kind with anything like fair margin.

---

[1] Dow's Theory.

But, suppose a trader, having a margin of two or three thousand dollars, wants to trade in and out of stocks without regard to values, but being governed by points or by impressions of what the general market is going to do. Experience has shown that such a trader will, in the end, profit by putting a stop order about 2 points from the price at which he goes in. If there is advice that a stock is going up and it instead goes down *2* points without some obviously good reason for such a decline, the advice was not good, and the quicker the speculator lets go the better.

It often happens that when a stock moves two points it moves more, and it is a peculiarity of the human mind to disregard a small loss, but to get frightened and take a large loss just when wisdom would call for averaging a purchase.

Thousands of traders have said at two points loss that they would see that particular transaction through if the stock went to nothing, only to decide after it had declined ten points that there was good reason for believing that it would decline ten more and acting accordingly. The experience of most traders is that the small losses occasioned by stop orders have a tendency to check their trading with a small aggregate loss, while the practice of letting a loss run not infrequently makes a loss so large that trading comes to an end because the speculator has no more money.

The maxim "let your profits run, but cut your losses short" has received the approval of most of the great stock operators. The authorship of the maxim has been credited to a dozen people, and most of them would have been willing to father it, although the great fortunes in stocks have not usually been made by people who give stop orders. Their opinions that stop orders were wise were based on their observation of people who tried to trade with insufficient capital, to whom stop orders especially apply.

The great profits in stocks have almost invariably been made by people who saw the tendency of events clearly, and who then bought a large amount of stock which they thought certain to get the results of great increase in prosperity. Such stock has either been paid for outright or very heavily margined, and then it has been held for months or years until great profits accrued.

Take the opportunities that have occurred in the last six years, or since 1896. Any one of from twenty to forty stocks could have been bought around 20 and sold above 80, and in at least half the cases above par, within that time. Such great opportunities do not come every year, but there are few times when some stocks cannot be pointed out as being lower in price than in value and as entitled to advance.

In a close speculative sense, a stop order is often useful. Stocks may be bought just when a reaction is setting in. In this case, it is frequently wise to take a quick loss on the theory that the reaction is likely to be 5 or 6 points, and that the stock can be recovered with a net saving of two or three points. A stop order is of use to out-of-town customers, because sometimes the market moves a good deal before a broker can communicate with his client and get an order to act. Stop orders are often valuable on the short side of the market, because a scare of shorts after considerable decline sometimes brings a very rapid rise, which runs away with all the profits that have accrued.

Customers who give stop orders should, however, understand exactly what they mean. A customer who, being long of Union Pacific at 105, should give an order to stop at 103, would in effect be saying to the broker: "Whenever Union Pacific sells at 103, sell my stock immediately at the best price obtainable."

If the best price obtainable were 102 or even 101, the broker would still be within his rights in executing the order. Hence, in giving stop orders, thought should be taken as to the size of the market in the stock. In Union Pacific, for instance, a stop order ought to be executed within ⅛ or ¼ per cent of the stop order price, except in cases of panic, but a stop order in Lackawanna or Chicago & Eastern Illinois or in some industrial stock would be very dangerous, because no approximate idea could be formed as to what price would have to be accepted.

Stop orders should not be given in any case in stocks of very limited market. In other stocks, their value will be found to depend largely upon the methods employed by the trader himself.

CHAPTER XI.

[1]CUTTING LOSSES SHORT.

We have spoken in previous articles of methods of trading. Experience proves that every operator should adopt one of two methods: Either cut losses short, or take an investment position. We propose to point out to-day some of the advantages of cutting losses short.

The buyer of any stock has some reason for his action. He has heard that the stock is going up; he believes that it is selling below its value, he sees that a bull market is under way and believes that this stock will go up as much as any other. These and similar reasons lead to buying.

It is obvious that in all but one of these cases the buyer does not profess to know anything definitely about the stock he buys. He acts on the suggestions or advice of others. Points are good when they are good, and under some conditions can very wisely be followed. There is nothing better in trading than to know that a great operator or a great syndicate intends for good reasons to move the price of a stock from a lower to a higher figure.

But almost everybody learns by sad experience that the "best laid plans of mice and men gang aft agley." Great operators change their minds about the expediency of market movements and most of them have learned that it is one thing to will and another to do in stock speculation. Hence the trader who takes a point, even from good sources, has only partial assurance of profitable results.

---

[1]   Dow's Theory.

37

His true protection in such a case lies in a stop order. If the price advances, well and good, but if it declines his stop order cuts his loss short, while those who do not stop the loss, but who listen to assurances that the market is all right, often see larger losses in the end.

The general rule is to stop losses within a range of two or three points from the purchase price. All purchases on points, tendencies and rumors should be regarded as guesses and protected by stop orders. Traders, looking over their accounts, seldom lament the losses of $200, which they find scattered through their books as the result of stops, but they deeply lament the $1,500 or the $2,500 losses which reflect over-confidence in a position which proved unsound.

The difficulty with stop orders is that they are frequently exercised when the event shows that the loss need not have been taken. There is no help for this, but the placing of a stop order can be wisely varied by the circumstances of a given case. Suppose, for instance, that the 5-year movement showed a bull market to be in progress; that there has come in this advance a 5-point reaction in a stock like Union Pacific and that a purchase had been made 5 points from the previous highest.

If the price declined 2 points more in such a case, it would probably be wise to exercise the stop order as the fall would suggest a downswing of larger proportions than had been anticipated. It might be such a move as occurred in December, 1899, when stop orders proved exceedingly profitable in bull accounts. If the price subsequently recovered the 2 points, and the stock was repurchased at about the original price, it would probably be wise to put the stop order the next time about 3 points away, under a belief that the stock would not go quite so low as it went before and that the stop order would therefore not be executed.

If this reasoning proved sound, and the price advanced, the

stop order could wisely be kept 3 points below the market price until the stock had advanced several points and showed signs of what is called "toppiness." Then it might be well to advance the stop order to 2 points and await developments. The stop order is of primary importance when a purchase is first made and when its wisdom is in doubt. It is also of primary importance in pyramiding; that is, where stock is being bought on an advancing market every point up, because in such a case the stop order is relied upon to prevent the turning of a profit into a loss. It is of importance when a stock has had its normal swing for the purpose of saving most of the profit if a reaction comes, while leaving a chance open for further advance. It is of least importance when a stock has been well bought and is slowly advancing. It should be set further away from the market at such a time than any other so as to avoid being caught on the small setbacks which occur in an advancing period.

By means of a stop order, an operator can trade freely in active stocks of uncertain value, which he would not venture to touch as an investment. By it, he can trade in much larger amounts than he could otherwise undertake to protect. The stop order is the friend of the active speculator, who wants to make a quick dash for a large profit and who is willing to make small losses in the hope of getting a good run once in four or five attempts. It is the friend of the small operator, the out-of-town operator and the timid operator. It should be applied, however, only in active stocks where there is a large market. Stop orders should not be given in inactive stocks, as the seller may be slaughtered in their execution.

A stop order to sell 100 shares of Union Pacific at 75 means that the stock must be sold at the best price obtainable as soon as there has been a transaction at 75. If the best price were 74 or 73, it would still be the duty of the broker to sell. Hence the importance of not giving such orders in stocks where wide differences in quotations may be expected.

CHAPTER XII.

[1]THE DANGER IN OVERTRADING.

Afrequent inquiry is: "Can I trade in stocks on a capital of $100, buying on a scale up and stopping my loss so as to protect my original capital?"

There are a great many people in the United States who think about trading in stocks on a capital of $100 or $200. Many of them believe that if a thousand dollars is a proper 10 per cent margin for trading in 100 shares, $100 must be à fair margin for trading in 10 shares. We regard this reasoning as sound, but dissent from the conclusion that $1,000 justifies trading in 100 share lots.

The reason is that nobody can hope to buy at the bottom or to sell at the top; or to be right all the time or to avoid losses. Making money in stocks for most people resolves itself into a series of transactions in which we may say there are six profits and four losses, resulting in a net gain. The experience of good traders shows that the operating expenses in trading, that is to say, the ratio of losses to profits, run from 50 to 65 per cent of the total profits.

A man who may have made $10,000 gross in trading in a specified time will be very likely to have lost from $5,000 to $6,000 gross in the same time, leaving a net profit of from $4,000 to $5,000. Profits and losses run in streaks. There will be times of all profit and no loss, and times of all loss and no profit. But the average even for those who have learned to trade in stocks and

---

[1]   Dow's Theory.

who have abundant capital for their operations works out less than half of the gross profits as net profits.

What chance is there for 10 per cent to carry a speculator and especially a beginner through the losses which are almost certain to come before he can accumulate any substantial profit? It is possible to say that if an operator had done this or that, buying at the right time and selling at the right time, 10 per cent would have been ample. But, there is a great difference between seeing what might have been done in the past and undertaking to do something for the future.

The man who wishes to trade in stocks and who has only $100 to lose, should, in our opinion, adopt one of two courses. He should buy outright one share of some stock below par and below its value and wait until the advance in that stock to its value gives him a profit of 5 or 10 per cent, as the case may be. This is probably the surest way.

The other way is to buy two or three shares on margin, protecting the account by a stop order at about two points from the purchase price. Brokers generally are not anxious to take such small lots, but if a broker believes that a customer is trading on right lines, and is likely to make money, he will go out of his way considerably to serve that customer under a belief that he will be worth something in the future. Nine brokers out of ten would say that an attempt to trade in stocks on a capital of $100 was absurd. But, it would not be absurd if the trading basis were made two shares, as that would give the trader time in which to recover from his losses as well as some confidence in acting at the proper time and would be a sort of school in which experience could be gained.

We think exactly the same reasoning holds good with regard to trading in 100-share lots on a basis of $1,000. Brokers accept such orders readily enough, but it is none the less over-trading, and none the less likely to result in the loss of the trader's capital. The man who buys 100 shares on a 10 per cent margin and stops his loss at 2 per cent has lost nearly one-quarter of his capital. He tries again and perhaps makes 1 per cent net. His third venture results in a loss of 3 per cent more and in a nearly total loss of confidence, leading him probably to sell short just when he ought to have averaged, thereby completing the sacrifice of his money.

If the same man with a capital of $1,000 had begun with 10 shares he could have stood his loss; he would have had courage to average or to buy something else at a low point and would very likely come out ahead.

Almost any man can show profits in stock by assuming that he would do so and so at various conditions of the market. He succeeds theoretically in this way because there is nothing at risk and his judgment is clear. The moment, however, that he has a risk which is very large in proportion to his capital, he consults his fears instead of his judgment, and does in practice exactly opposite what he would have done had his transactions been purely academic.

The remedy for this is to keep transactions down to a point, as compared with capital, which leaves the judgment clear and affords ample ability to cut loss after loss short; to double up; to take hold of something else, and generally to act easily and fearlessly instead of under the constraint which inevitably comes from a knowledge that the margin of safety is so small as to leave no room for anything except a few anxious gasps before the account is closed.

If people with either large or small capital would look upon trading in stocks as an attempt to get 12 per cent per annum on their money instead of 50 per cent weekly, they would come out a good deal better in the long run. Everybody knows this in its application to his private business, but the man who is prudent and careful in carrying on a store, a factory or a real estate business seems to think that totally different methods should be employed in dealing in stocks. Nothing is further from the truth.

CHAPTER XIII.

[1]METHODS OF TRADING.

A correspondent inquires: "How can a man living at a distance from Wall Street hope to follow the market closely enough to make any money trading in stocks?"

This question comes to us in different forms frequently, and shows misapprehensions as to what is involved in successful trading. Many people seem to think that if an operator is in Wall Street, he can tell what the market is going to do. Nothing is further from the fact. The more a man really knows about speculation, the less certain he becomes in regard to any market movement, except as the result of general conditions.

The distinction to be made between trading in the Street and trading from out of town is clear in one point. The operator who watches the ticker or blackboard can turn at very short notice, but the ability to turn quickly often proves a great disadvantage, because it leads to many turns at the wrong time.

The out of town speculator should not attempt to make quick turns, unless by private wire connections he is able to watch the market as a matter of business. The out of town operator should trade on broad lines and from an investment standpoint. He should deal not in stocks that happen to be active and not on points but almost wholly on well considered convictions as to the probable course of the general market and the relative position of price to value of the special stocks in which he proposes to deal.

---

[1] Dow's Theory.

The first question to consider is what constitutes a speculative investment. We should say it meant in most cases a railway stock paying regular dividends, publishing earnings gross and net at regular intervals and giving full particulars of its financial and physical condition as often at least as once a year. If oftener, so much the better.

It is possible to derive fairly accurate knowledge of the value of such a stock. It should be considered essentially with reference to its ability to maintain or increase its dividends. If the stock seems likely to continue a current rate of dividend, and the return on the cost is such as to make it fairly satisfactory as an investment, it is a good stock to buy when, in sympathy with decline in the general market, it has fallen below its normal price.

Take, for instance, Union Pacific common. A few months ago this stock was selling between 50 and 60. It was paying 4 per cent dividends, and the company was known to be earning over 8 per cent. Here was the case of a stock obviously selling below its value. It has since risen more than 30 points. There were other stocks, perhaps not as cheap in point of value, but of which, much that was favorable could be said. Three months ago the values of railway stocks generally were above their prices.

Now, this can be said of very few stocks, and this fact ought to make an outsider slow to buy. The chances are that there will come, as there seems to be coming, declines which will carry prices back to a level where it will again be prudent to buy. Suppose that time to arrive. The wise course for an outsider will be to buy of a good railroad stock, an amount he can easily purchase outright, and which he would be willing to hold as an investment in case the price should decline. Should it then decline considerably it would probably be prudent for him to buy more, lowering his average, but only after careful revision of the facts bearing upon the value and upon the general market.

This stock should be held without regard to current fluctuations, until it showed a satisfactory profit. Then it should be sold and the operator should wait weeks or months if necessary for an opportunity to take it or some other stock back upon favorable terms.

The outsider, who tries to follow the market from day to day, is not likely to have very marked success. The operator who selects investment properties carefully and buys after the market has had general declines, and who exercises a good deal of patience both in waiting for the time to buy and for the time to sell—who, in short, treats his speculation as an investment, will be likely to make money in stocks as a rule.

A correspondent writes: "Is there any way by which an outsider who cannot watch fluctuations of the market hourly can trade in stocks with a fair chance of making money?"

We think there are two methods by either of which an outsider has a fair speculative chance. The first is to buy stocks for investment; that is, to pay for them outright when they are selling below value and wait until they are up to value, getting the difference for a profit.

Value is determined by the margin of safety over dividends, the size and tendency of earnings: the soundness of the balance sheet and of operating methods, and general prospects for the future. This sounds rather complicated, but is not especially difficult to work out.

For instance, a year ago we almost daily pointed out that earnings had greatly increased during the year past; that fixed charges had not increased, hence that the actual value of stocks had advanced while prices had in most cases declined. It was obvious that this could not last; that net earnings must decrease or prices advance. There were then many stocks cheap on their earnings and this was easily a matter of demonstration.

In the same sense it can now (1902) be said that most stocks are dear on their earnings. It is true that earnings have increased somewhat over last year, but prices of many stocks have advanced from 50 to 100 per cent, and in whatever form the yardstick is applied the result is unfavorable to value as compared with prices in a large number of the active stocks.

When a stock sells at a price which returns only about 3½ per cent on the investment, it is obviously dear, except there be some special reason for the established price. In the long run, the prices of stocks adjust themselves to the return on the investment and while this is not a safe guide at all times it is a guide that should never be laid aside or overlooked. The tendency of prices over a considerable length of time will always be toward values. Therefore, the outsider who by studying earning conditions can approach a fairly correct idea of value has a guide for his investments which will, as a whole, be found safe.

Most people, however, when they talk about making money in stocks do not mean the slow road through investments but the short cut by way of speculation. We think here again there is one rule worth all others on this subject. It is a rule which is carried out with greater or less precision by a majority of successful traders. It has been approved by the great masters of speculation and it is indorsed by the practical experience of almost everybody who has dealt at all freely in stocks.

This rule is to cut losses short but let profits run. It sounds very easy to follow, but is in reality difficult to observe. The difficulty arises from the unwillingness of an operator to take a small loss when experience shows him that in many cases such a loss need not have been taken. Furthermore, the practice of this rule suggests that having, for instance, bought a stock and taken a loss, the stock should be bought again, and this may have to be done three or four times before an advance finally comes.

These three or four losses prove very burdensome and lead people oftentimes to decide not to cut the loss short and that is generally when a large loss ensues.

The question will of course be asked whether there should be a uniform stop loss, or whether it should vary with varying conditions. Experience indicates that two points is the wisest place to stop a loss. If a stock goes two points against the buyer, it is very liable to go more, and it suggests that the expected move has either been delayed or is not coming.

Suppose, for instance, that an operator believes from information, study of values, experience in markets and the tendency of the period that Union Pacific ought to be bought at 107. If he buys at that price and the stock falls to 105, theoretically he should cut his loss, buying it again when the indications are again favorable.

Extended records of trading show that this policy, blindly followed, with blind following also of the plan of letting profits run, would give better results than most people are able to obtain by the exercise of judgment. At the same time, judgment can sometimes be wisely employed in cutting a loss.

It is not, for instance, necessary in all cases to take a loss because the price is suddenly jammed down 2 points. If the market shows a tendency to rally, wait a little. If a decline in the stock bought is obviously due to a collapse in some other stock, and that collapse seems to have spent its force, it would be unnecessary to execute the stop. The idea is to stop the loss when the market has legitimately declined to that extent.

In letting profits run there are two ways of determining when to close. One is to wait until the general market shows a decided change of temper. The other is to keep a stop order about 3 points behind the high prices on the advance and close on that stop. Here, again, experience has shown that when a stock starts on a manipulated advance, it is seldom allowed to react as much as 3 points until the move is completed. If it reacts 3 points, it may mean trouble with the deal, although there are cases where such reactions are allowed for the purpose of shaking out following. Here, again, something can be left to judgment.

But the great thing is having bought a stock and having got fairly away from the purchase price, not to be in too great a hurry about selling, provided that the general market is bullish. In a bear market, the whole proceeding ought to be reversed, the operator taking the short side instead of the long, but in other respects applying the same rule.

We do not wish to be understood as saying that there is any sure way of making money in stocks, but the principle of buying after a period of steadiness in prices, stopping losses and letting profits run will, as a matter of statistical record, beat most people's guessing at what is going to occur.

CHAPTER XIV.

[1]THE OUT OF TOWN TRADER.

A correspondent asks: "How can a man living at an interior city, where he sees quotations only once or twice a day, make money by trading in stocks?"

This question touches a point which seems to find widespread acceptance, namely, that proximity to Wall Street is a special advantage in trading. It certainly is for some kinds of trading. If a man owns a seat on the Stock Exchange and pays no commissions, he can probably do best by operating for his own account on the floor of the exchange, although not every man with these facilities is able to make his profits exceed his losses.

For practical purposes, it may be said that most traders in or out of Wall Street are handicapped by the commission of $25 for buying and selling 100 shares of stock. There probably are some evasions of the commission rule, but as far as individual operators are concerned commissions are not much evaded.

A commission of $12.50 for buying and as much more for selling 100 shares of stock is insignificant if there are ten or even five points difference between the buying and selling price. But the commission is serious if the difference between the buying and the selling price is only one point. A man who started in to trade for one point profit and pays ⅛ commission would inevitably give all his money to his broker in the course of time.

The ordinary operator must always endeavor to get comparatively large profits. He should not buy unless he feels warranted in believing that the stock which he selects will go

---

[1] Dow's Theory.

up four or five points, so that when he makes he will get double his loss when he loses. In trading for five or ten point turns, the operator at an interior city has one advantage. He does not hear the rumors and see sudden movements in prices which are the bane of the office trader.

Wall Street is often full of people to-day who have been long of the market for a month, but who have made little or no money, because they have been scared out by rumors and by small relapses. The man who does not see the market escapes this. The greatest advantage resting upon the out of town operator is the fact that sometimes the market will change its character so rapidly as to convert a profit into a loss or establish a loss larger than he intended to take before he knows it. This, however, does not occur as frequently as most people seem to suppose.

It is rather exceptional for the market, having run several points in one direction, to reverse the movement suddenly and without considerable fluctuations near the turning points. Such cases do occur, but they are unusual. After a 5-point rise, a stock usually has a period during which fluctuations are narrow and which are maintained long enough to give the out-of-town trader plenty of time to get out if he dislikes the appearance of the trading. Stop orders are the special protection of the out-of-town trader, who, if he will stick to stable stocks, can almost always cut his loss or save his profit at any spot where he deems wise.

The out-of-town trader wants to begin his campaign with a conviction that the stock which he buys is selling below its value. This should not only be a conviction, but a demonstrated conviction, which cannot be shaken if, at the outset, the price declines instead of advances. Having determined on his stock from the viewpoint of value, he should, if possible, wait about buying until the general market has had its normal setback from a high point.

If twenty active stocks have advanced 10 points, a normal setback would be four points, and then, in an extended period of rising prices, would be the time to make the initial purchase. The operator should then take in a great stock of patience. He will see other stocks go up and his stock stand still. He will see and hear daily that something else is making riches for traders, but he must shut his ears to these statements, even if they are right as far as fluctuations go. He must just sit on his stock, which is intrinsically below its value, until the other people observe that it is selling too low and begin to buy it or manipulate it.

The tendency with most people holding a stock which does not move for a time is to sell the stock about as soon as it begins to move, through fear that it will again become dull. This is just the time not to sell, but, if anything, to buy more on the idea that other people have discovered that the price is below value. After the price has moved up two or three points, it is well to put in a stop order perhaps two points back from the top and follow the rise in the stock with the stop order disregarding current reports and waiting until the price is either up to the value or until market conditions make taking a profit judicious, provided always that a sudden setback does not close out the transaction.

An out-of-town operator can do all this just as well as an office trader and in some respects better. Some of the large operators like to go away from the market and work from Newport or Saratoga or other distant points in order to look at the trading with an unbiased mind and without being unsettled by the rumors that always grow out of any special move. The outsider who will wisely study values and market conditions and then exercise patience enough for six men will be likely to make money in stocks.

CHAPTER XV.

[1]THE SHORT SIDE OF THE MARKET.

A correspondent writes: "You demonstrate that an operator in stocks ought to work on the short side of the market during about half of almost every decade. I feel some hesitation about selling property which I do not own. Will you not make it clear how the short side of the market is normal trading?"

It is quite true that in each of the past four decades it would have been wise to have worked on the short side at least half of the time. It is also true that the public as a whole does not like short selling. It is true that corners occur at long intervals and are destructive to those caught therein. But they occur so seldom as to make them a very remote danger. There is about one in ten years.

We have explained the principle of short selling many times, but will state the process once more. A customer X directs Broker A to sell short 100 shares of Union Pacific at par. Broker B buys it. A, not having the stock goes to Broker C, and borrows from him 100 shares of Union Pacific, giving as security $10,000 in cash. This stock is then delivered by A to B, who pays A $10,000 therefore. Matters then rest until Union Pacific advances or declines enough to make X wish to close his account, He then directs A to buy Union Pacific, say at 95, and A gets the stock from Broker D. The stock thus obtained is delivered to C, who thereupon returns the money which he has had as security and

---

[1] Dow's Theory.

$9,500 of the amount goes to D, leaving $500, less expenses, as the profit of X on the transaction.

While X is waiting to see what the market is going to do C has the use of A's $10,000, and under ordinary conditions, pays interest on this money. This interest is called the loaning rate on stocks and is usually a little below the current rate for loans on collateral.

The lower these rates are, compared with the rate for money, the more demand there is to borrow that particular stock, and the loaning rate is the point to be watched by those who may be short, to see whether the short interest is large or small.

In case the demand to borrow a certain stock is very large, the loaning rate will be quoted flat, which means in the case cited that C would get the use of A's $10,000 without paying any interest. If the demand for the stock should be still greater, A might have not only to give C the $10,000 without interest, but pay C a small premium in addition. When the loaning rate of a stock is quoted at 1-32 it means that C gets his $10,000 from A, without interest, and in addition a premium of $3.12 a day for each 100 shares, which has to be paid by X, who must also pay all dividends that may be declared on the stock.

In ordinary lines of business, selling short with the idea of borrowing for delivery would be impossible. In the stock market it is impracticable to sell distributed bonds or investment stocks short because such securities are held by investors, and are not carried in quantity by brokers, hence, could not be readily borrowed. But, in active stocks, there is no difficulty whatever in borrowing.

The reason is this: Every broker who carries many stocks employs a great deal more money than he possesses. In theory, a broker carrying for a customer 100 shares of Union Pacific at par would make up the money for the purchase by using $1,000 belonging to the customer, $1,000 of the money of the brokerage firm, and then borrowing $8,000 from a bank on the security of the 100 shares of stock purchased.

An active broker, consequently, is always a large borrower of money, and when he borrows from a bank he is expected to put up 20 per cent margin on his loan. But if he can lend stocks he gets the full value of the stock and does not have to put up any of his own money or of his customer's money. Hence, every broker is willing to lend stocks, particularly when the demand for stock is sufficient to make the rate of interest lower than the market rate, as the broker in this case makes a profit by charging his customer who is long 5 or 6 per cent interest, while he perhaps secures his money without any cost through lending the stock flat.

This, from the standpoint of the short seller, is what makes his operation practically safe. Ordinarily, it is just as easy to borrow active stocks as it is to borrow money, and squeezes of shorts through inability to borrow are little if any more frequent than squeezes of "longs" through the difficulty of brokers in borrowing money.

Squeezes of shorts sometimes develop themselves and are sometimes manipulated. When friends of a property see a large short interest they sometimes try to persuade holders of the stock to agree not to lend it for a day or two and thus scare shorts to cover by difficulty in borrowing. If this undertaking is successful brokers are notified to return borrowed stock, and when they try to borrow elsewhere they find little offering. The loaning rate possibly runs up to ¼ per cent a day, or perhaps higher.

Shorts are alarmed and cover, advancing the price of the stock and enabling holders to sell at a profit. Such a squeeze usually lasts only two or three days, as by that time the advanced price leads those who have the stock to either sell it or lend it, and the price then usually goes lower than before. Sometimes there is a short interest so large and so persistent as to keep a stock lending at a premium for some time. This is usually almost certain evidence of decline, but the expenses of premiums and the necessity of paying dividends sometimes eat up the profits so that but little remains even after considerable fall in price. Mr. Gould is said to have once remained short of New York Central over four years, and to have had a large profit as between his buying and his selling price, but to have had the greater part of it eaten up in dividends.

In picking out a stock to sell short, the first consideration ought to be that the price is above value, and that future value appears to be shrinking. It should be an active stock and, if possible, a stock of large capital. It should be an old stock by preference, which means having wide distribution instead of concentrated ownership. By preference it should be a high priced stock with a reasonable probability that dividends will be reduced or passed. Such a stock should be sold on advances and bought in on moderate declines, say 4 or 5 points, as long as the market seems to be reasonably steady. But, if the market becomes distinctly weak, only part of the short stock should be bought in with the hope that some short interest may be established at a price so high as to be out of reach of temporary swings. The best profits in the stock market are made by people who get long or short at extremes and stay for months or years before they take their profit.

CHAPTER XVI.

[1]SPECULATION FOR THE DECLINE.

T he question is frequently asked whether in taking a bearish view of the general market it is expected that all stocks will go down together or that some will fall and others not.

The answer to this question takes two forms—the first is the speculative movement; the second the effect of values. When the market goes down, especially if the decline is violent or continued, all stocks fall; not perhaps equally, but enough to be regarded as participating fully in a general decline. Indeed, it often happens that a stock of admitted large value will fall more in a panic than a stock of little value.

The reason is that when people have been carrying various stocks, some good and some bad, and a time comes when they are obliged to suddenly furnish additional margin or reduce their commitments, they try to sell the stocks for which they think the market will be best, namely, their best stocks. But the very merit of such stocks prevents the existence of a short interest, hence when considerable amounts are offered in a panic there is no demand for covering purposes, and, in fact, no demand except from investors who may not know of the decline or who may not have money for investment at that particular moment. Consequently the good stock drops until it meets an investment demand somewhere. This condition was illustrated by the action of Delaware & Hudson in the panic of May 9, 1901. It had nearly, if not quite, the largest decline of any stock on the list, falling in

---

[1]   Dow's Theory.

half an hour from 160 to 105, chiefly because people generally did not know the price at which stock was being offered.

It may be accepted, therefore, that in a general decline, merit in a stock will not count for the time being. Good and bad will decline measurably alike. But here comes in a marked distinction. When the recovery comes, a day or a week later, the good stock will recover more and hold its recovery better than the poor stock. Delaware & Hudson is again a good illustration. After the quotation of 105 was printed on May 9 orders to buy the stock came from all sections, and in another hour the price was in the neighborhood of 150.

Value will always work out in the course of time. A stock intrinsically cheap and a stock intrinsically dear may be selling at the same price at a given time. As the result of six months' trading they may have presented the appearance of moving together in most of the fluctuations, but at the end of the period the good stock will be 10 points higher than the poor one, the difference representing a little smaller decline and a little better rally in each of five or six swings.

This exactly describes what will occur all through the market during the next bear period, whenever that period comes. There will be a sifting of the better from the worse, visible enough at a distance, but not conspicuous at any particular stage in the process.

Where there is a great change in the value of a stock it will advance in a bear period. The market as a whole declined from 1881 to 1885, but in that period Manhattan, while participating in most of the market swings, went from the neighborhood of 30 to the neighborhood of par, because the increased earnings of the company increased value steadily and largely during that time.

The practical lesson is that a stock operator should not deal in stocks unless he thinks he knows their value, nor unless he can watch conditions so as to recognize changes in value as they come along. He should then have at least a conviction as to what stocks are above their value and what are below their value at a given time. If the main tendency of the market is downward, he should sell stocks which he believes to be above their value when they are very strong, taking them in on the next general decline. In buying for a rally, he should invariably take the stocks that are below their value, selling them also when a moderate profit is shown.

When the market appears in a doubtful position it is sometimes wise to sell short a stock that is conspicuously above its value and buy a stock which is conspicuously below its value, believing that one will protect the other until the position of the general market becomes clear. It was formerly very popular for traders to be long of Northwest and short of St. Paul, usually with good results.

During the past year (1901-2) there have been operators who have aimed to be long of Manhattan and short of either Metropolitan or Brooklyn on the same line of reason. The general method of operating such an account is to trade for the difference; that is, supposing a transaction to have been started with the two stocks 10 points apart—the account is closed when they are, say, 15 points apart, assuring 5 points net profit. It is all, however, a part of the same general law. Stocks fluctuate together, but prices are controlled by values in the long run.

CHAPTER XVII.

[1]CONCERNING DISCRETIONARY ACCOUNTS.

A correspondent writes: "I inclose herewith a circular in which the sender asks me to give him a discretionary account promising large returns and claiming great success in past operations. A man in the market ought to be able to do better for me than I could do for myself at a distance. Is this party reliable, and do you consider his scheme safe?"

We get this letter in some form very often and have answered it many times, but it is difficult to make people see the truth. Outsiders want to make money and they believe that people in Wall Street know what the market is going to do, hence that the only question involved in discretionary accounts is the honesty of the men who run them.

The fact is that people in Wall Street, even those who get very near the center of large operations, do not know what the market is going to do with any regularity or certainty. The more they actually know, the less confident they become, and the large operators who try to make markets are, in most cases, the least confident of anybody because they know so well the variety and extent of the difficulties which may be encountered.

People who trade in stocks can set down as a fundamental proposition the fact that any man who claims to know what the market is going to do any more than to say that he thinks this or that will occur as a result of certain specified conditions is unworthy of trust as a broker. Any man who claims that he can take discretionary accounts and habitually make money for his

---

[1]   Dow's Theory.

customers, is a fraud; first, because he knows when he makes such statements that he cannot do it regularly or with certainty, and, second, because if he could, he would surely trade for himself and would scorn working for ⅛ commission when he could just as well have the whole amount made.

The governors of the Stock Exchange will not permit a member of that body to advertise that he will take discretionary accounts, and any Stock Exchange member who stated that he was endeavoring to build up a business by discretionary trading for customers would lose caste with his fellow-members. It would be considered that he was either lacking in honesty or in judgment.

We do not say that Stock Exchange houses never take a discretionary account. They sometimes do, but they take them unwillingly in very limited amounts, only for people with whom they have very confidential relations and who understand speculation sufficiently to expect losses and failures quite as frequently as profits. It is safe to say that Stock Exchange houses regard the acceptance of a discretionary account as a rather serious demand upon personal friendship, and this not because they do not wish to see their friends make money, but because they know too well that a discretionary account often means the loss of both money and friends.

When, therefore, men of little or no capital and little or no reputation advertise boldly in the Sunday papers that they desire discretionary accounts from strangers and will, for a commission of ⅛ per cent, guarantee profits ranging from 25 to 250 per cent per annum, commission houses have but one word with which to describe the proposition and people of practical experience in Wall Street are amazed at the credulity of those who send their money to be placed in such accounts and who subsequently appear in the company of those who wail in the outer rooms of closed offices over the rascality which has robbed them of their hard earnings.

The head of a discretionary concern which was very prominent a year or two ago frequently said that if the United States Government would let his mails alone and deliver to him the money forwarded by his dupes he would ask no better occupation and no quicker road to wealth. Evidence presented in court has shown repeatedly that swindlers who have advertised to make money for the public in speculation have received thousands of letters containing money; that none of this money was ever invested in stocks; that the advertisers were not members of any exchange and did not even pretend to have any business other than receiving and keeping the bulk of the money entrusted to their care. A small amount of the money received was usually returned to senders as profits on alleged transactions.

This is substantially, we believe, the general practice. If a man sends $100 to one of the concerns, he is notified, after a little time, that he has made $10 and, a little later, that his share of a pool profit is $15. At this point he is usually advised to send $100 more on account of some extraordinary opportunity which has just arisen. If this money is sent, he is told that profits have accrued and still more money is called for. Persons who call for some of their profits are occasionally given money in order that the receiver may induce others to join the list of future victims.

The end, however, is almost, if not quite invariably, a communication stating that by some adverse and utterly unexpected fatality operations have been unsuccessful and the money invested has been lost. It is usually thought wise to make the victims appear somewhat in debt in order to induce them by not having to pay the alleged debt to accept as a mysterious dispensation of Providence the loss of their capital and previous alleged profits.

Speculation is not at its best a simple and easy road to wealth, but speculation through people who advertise guaranteed profits and who call for participation in blind pools is as certain a method of loss as could possibly be discovered. The mere fact that a man openly asks for such accounts is the most ample and exhaustive reason possible for declining to give them.

CHAPTER XVIII.

[1]THE LIABILITY FOR LOSS.

O f a number of inquiries lately the following is a sample: "I was long of stocks May 9, 1901, and was sold out. The broker now asks me to pay a loss in excess of my margin. Am I liable therefore?"

This question has never been definitely settled as a matter of law. There have been a good many decisions in cases of this kind but they have generally been sufficiently dissimilar to make each decision rest upon that particular case, and not as establishing a principle of law, bearing thereon. The courts have shown a disposition to rule that in such cases trade customs must be considered and that such customs while not making the law, affect the bearing of the law thereon.

Cases of this kind generally fall under one of two general divisions. Either the broker notifies his customer that his margin is nearly exhausted, or he does not. It is probably good law to assume that where a stock is bought on margin and, on a fall in the price, the broker calls on the customer for more margin and there is no response within a reasonable time, the broker is justified in selling the stock without a positive order to do so from the customer. The courts have held in such cases that the broker gave ample notice and the customer should have responded in time to protect his interests. The broker could not be expected to wait more than a reasonable time.

In cases of this class it sometimes happens that the customer does not think it wise to put up more margin and orders the

---

[1] Dow's Theory.

stock sold. It may be sold at a loss on account of a rapid decline in prices. In this case, there seems to be little doubt of the liability of the customer, because the broker is executing an order to sell for the account and risk of that customer. Here, however, might enter special questions as to whether the broker was or was not negligent in notifying the customer that margin was needed, or in the execution of the order when it was received, or in some other respect whereby the interest of the customer was allowed to suffer.

The other general class of cases is where margin on accounts is swept away by a sudden decline and the broker faces the question whether it is better to sell his customer's stock without an order or to endeavor to carry the customer through the decline with the expectation that the loss, if there is a loss, will be made good by the customer.

The tendency of decisions in these cases is toward holding the broker to rather close accountability for his actions. The point has been made that the broker in such a case is acting in a double capacity. First, as a broker executing an order for a customer for a commission. Second, as a banker in making a loan to this customer, being protected therein by the security of money deposited and the possession of the stock purchased. As a broker, the equity might be one way, while as a banker it might be exactly opposite.

Generally speaking, a banker has no right to sell out a loan without notifying the borrower, except where there has been a special agreement permitting such action. This fact leads banks and institutions in nearly all cases to make loans with a formal agreement authorizing them to sell the collateral at their option in case the loan ceases to be satisfactory. As a matter of practice, banks call for more collateral when prices decline. But in cases of panic or the inability of brokers to furnish more collateral, loans are frequently sold out, under the special agreement to that effect.

Some commission houses protect themselves by a formal agreement with customers similar to that required by banks. When a customer opens an account, he signs an agreement authorizing the broker to sell the stock bought at his discretion in case the margin runs down to the danger line.

This is undoubtedly a wise method, as it removes all doubt as to the position of each party in the premises. Such agreements are not invariably made because in the competition for business brokers do not like to impose restrictions which are not universal and which may have a tendency to drive away customers. Nevertheless, experiences like those of the 9th of May have a decided tendency toward defining the relations between broker and customer.

The action of the market May 9 was so rapid as to make it impossible for a broker to notify a customer of the need of more margin and get a response in time to be of any use. A 10-point margin was of no use at a time when stocks were falling 10 points in five minutes. There were many cases that day in which wealthy commission houses saw a large percentage of their capital disappear in customers' accounts between 11 and 11.30. The rapidity of the recovery was all that saved multitudes of customers and many commission houses. Loans, small and large, were unsound and sound again before lenders had time to sell even if they had been disposed to do so.

There were, however, many cases where stocks were sold entailing large losses and the location of these losses is in a number of cases still in legal controversy, with the probability that the decision will turn more or less upon the circumstances peculiar to each case. The 9th of May was a very extraordinary day and allowance must be made for its unusual character. Stock

Exchange rules based on the occurrences of the 9th of May would prohibit doing business under ordinary conditions, but such days come and on this account brokers and customers should make provision for the unexpected by a clear understanding as to what shall be done in emergencies.

It is often difficult to say what shall be done when a loss has occurred through unusual conditions and under circumstances which made the action taken largely discretionary. This fact in its application to the May panic has led brokers and customers in cases to adopt a policy of trying to divide the loss equitably and with due reference to the facts involved in that particular case. A jury familiar with Stock Exchange business would be very likely to render a decision along somewhat similar lines.

CHAPTER XIX.

[1]THE RECURRENCE OF CRISES.

A correspondent writes: "Is it true that commercial or stock exchange panics are approximately periodic in their occurrence?"

The facts point distinctly in that direction, and there is reason back of the facts. The reason is that the business community has a tendency to go from one extreme to the other. As a whole, it is either contracting business under a belief that prices will be lower or expanding under a belief that prices will be higher. It appears to take ordinarily five or six years for public confidence to go from the point of too little hope to the point of too much confidence and then five or six years more to get back to the condition of hopelessness.

This ten-year movement in England is given in detail by Professor Jevons in his attempt to show that sun spots have some bearing upon commercial affairs. Without going into the matter of sun spots and their bearing upon crops, commerce, or states of minds, it may be assumed that Professor Jevons has stated correctly the periods of depression as they have occurred in England during the last two centuries.

The dates given by him as the years in which commercial crises have occurred follow: 1701, 1711, 1712, 1731-2, 1742, 1752, 1763, 1772-3, 1783, 1793, 1804-5, 1815, 1825, 1836, 1847, 1857, 1866 and 1878.

---

[1]   Dow's Theory.

This makes a very good showing for the ten-year theory, and it is supported to a considerable extent by what has occurred in this country during the past century.

The first crisis in the United States during the nineteenth century came in 1814, and was precipitated by the capture of Washington by the British on the 24th of August in that year. The Philadelphia and New York banks suspended payments, and for a time the crisis was acute. The difficulties leading up to this period were the great falling off in foreign trade caused by the embargo and non-intercourse acts of 1808, the excess of public expenditures over public receipts, and the creation of a large number of state banks taking the place of the old United States bank. Many of these state banks lacked capital and issued currency without sufficient security.

There was a near approach to a crisis in 1819 as the result of a tremendous contraction of bank circulation. The previous increases of bank issues had promoted speculation; the contraction caused a serious fall in the prices of commodities and real estate. This, however, was purely a money panic as far as its causes were concerned.

The European crisis in 1825 caused a diminished demand for American products and led to lower prices and some money stringency in 1826. The situation, however, did not become very serious and was more in the nature of an interruption to progress than a reversal of conditions.

The year 1837 brought a great commercial panic, for which there was abundant cause. There had been rapid industrial and commercial growth, with a multitude of enterprises established ahead of the time. Crops were deficient, and breadstuffs were imported. The refusal of the government to extend the charter of the United States Bank had caused a radical change in the banking business of the country, while the withdrawal of public deposits and their lodgment with state banks had given the foundation for abnormal speculation.

The panic in Europe in 1847 exerted but little influence in this country, although there was a serious loss in specie, and the Mexican war had some effect in checking enterprises. These effects, however, were neutralized somewhat by large exports of breadstuffs and later by the discovery of gold in 1848-9.

There was a panic of the first magnitude in 1857, following the failure of the Ohio Life Insurance & Trust Company in August. This panic came unexpectedly, although prices had been falling for some months. There had been very large railroad building, and the proportion of specie held by banks was very small in proportion to their loans and deposits. One of the features of this period was the great number of failures. The banks generally suspended payments in October.

The London panic in 1866 precipitated by the failure of Overend, Guerney & Co., was followed by a heavy fall in prices in the Stock Exchange here. In April there had been a corner in Michigan Southern and rampant speculation generally, from which the relapse was rather more than normal.

The panic of September, 1873, was a commercial as well as a Stock Exchange panic. It was the outcome of an enormous conversion of floating into fixed capital. Business had been expanded on an enormous scale, and the supply of money became insufficient for the demands made upon it. Credit collapsed and the depression was extremely serious.

The year 1884 brought a Stock Exchange smash but not a commercial crisis. The failure of the Marine Bank, Metropolitan Bank and Grant & Ward in May was accompanied by a large fall in prices and a general check which was felt throughout the year. The Trunk Line war, which had lasted for several years, was one of the factors in this period.

The panic of 1893 was the outcome of a number of causes—uncertainty in regard to the currency situation, the withdrawal of foreign investments and the fear of radical tariff legislation. The anxiety in regard to the maintenance of the gold standard was undoubtedly the chief factor, as it bore upon many others.

Judging by the past and by the developments of the last six years, it is not unreasonable to suppose that we may get at least a stock exchange flurry in the next few years. This decade seems to be the one for the small crisis instead of the large one—a type of 1884 rather than a recurrence of 1837, 1873 or 1893.

CHAPTER XX.

FINANCIAL CRITICISM.

The stock market and its relation to newspapers is a much misunderstood subject. With the great increase in speculation and public interest, the newspapers have responded to a demand which, all things considered, is filled most creditably. It is only a few years ago that opening, high, and low quotations were considered sufficient to satisfy those interested in the stock market and for forty years there had been no improvement. This primitive method was superseded by a careful compilation of the day's trading, printed in tabulated form and including every sale made or transacted from the ticker, reproduced in an afternoon paper and sold on the street for a penny twenty minutes after the closing of the Stock Exchange. This remarkable development in the way of newspaper enterprise was made possible by the present owner of *The Sun* and *The Evening Sun* of New York, who was quick to realize the value to the public of such a service at the astonishing cost of the country's smallest coin. And so accurate has that service been that it has been accepted in courts of law as official in lieu of any better or as good service from the Stock Exchange itself.

Each newspaper supports a staff in Wall Street and the Street itself is represented by two reputable news bureaus a number of daily financial newspapers and several weeklies.

Stock market criticism is dependent largely upon the individual point of view of the writer and the policy of the newspaper itself. An afternoon newspaper market review may be an academic study of the money market, with the Stock Exchange subordinated to its relative position in the perspective, or it may be a simple review of the influential news factors that caused market fluctuations, and explanations reduced to common sense. Or it may pursue a middle course, indulging in economic speculations and at the same time not losing sight of the important fact that the reader wishes to know why particular stocks advanced or declined. A writer may be ultra-conservative and pessimistic as distinguished from the majority who are given to prophecy and inclined to optimism. And again he may be honest or corrupt, moral conditions that are governed by the individual and his environment.

The reliable critic usually endeavors to avoid the field of prophecy. It is almost invariably the fact that in reviewing the factors governing the situation he will endeavor to make bullish deductions; that is to say, he is prejudiced in favor of advancing security prices and the prosperity of those who own them. This is a natural position and one which meets with the approval of the reader. He is from necessity committed to the constructive side.

There are times, though, when his judgment enables him to detect the approaching financial storm and sound a note of warning. There are writers who see so many dangers in stock speculation and in the tendency to human excesses that scarcely a day passes that they do not justifiably condemn the market in one phase or another. And there are others, corrupted by their own speculations or the gratuities of stock manipulators, who pen grossly inaccurate and deceptive articles for pecuniary gain.

A market review is entitled to consideration to the extent that it is reasonable and accurate. If it is unreasonable, inaccurate and perhaps too radical in departing from established rules and customs it should be ignored. Per contra the opposite qualities should make it worthy of consideration.

Corrupt and inspired articles are readily detected. Should the alleged facts not be verified; should the prophet prove to be a false prophet; should the hand of the press-agent be in plain view, know then that you are following an unreliable and dishonest guide.

The usual method employed in corrupting the financial critic is for a stock manipulator to offer the disseminator of news, views and tips, a "Call" on a specified number of shares. Should a pool have a deal in view intending to advance a particular stock it will endeavor to obtain the support of those newspaper writers who will lend their columns and their newspapers to the legitimate or illegitimate movement, as the case may be, for a speculative opportunity to participate in a small way in the profits.

The representative of the pool proceeds in one of two ways. He will send (1) for the individual writer and offer him a "Call" on the stock under manipulation at a price. This price is usually above the market. In return the writer agrees to "boom" or "apply the hot air method" as it is required; or in simpler terms print misleading statements to facilitate the sale of stocks to its readers. A "Call" in such a proposition would mean that the writer received the privilege of calling upon the manipulator for a specified number of shares of stock at a certain price. If the stock declined the privilege would have no monetary value. If the stock advanced the writer could sell the stock against the "Call" and receive the difference between the price written on the "Call" and the price at which the stock was sold, or the transaction would be closed in the manner most acceptable to the man who had paid the bribe.

Or (2) the manipulator may send for one newspaper writer, who in turn represents a combination of writers, and give the newspaper man complete charge of the transaction and the power to distribute the "Calls" as, in his judgment, he considers that the best results can be obtained. Some of these "Calls" are very profitable and others quite worthless. They may be repudiated at any time and their holders have no redress or claim. Their owners are powerless to antagonize the interest which deceived them, for publicity means exposure, and exposure ruin.

It must be conceded, however, that where this form of corruption exists it is readily detected and that all things considered the newspaper protects the public better than the public are at times willing to acknowledge. The majority of the Wall Street financial writers are honest men and will freely sacrifice the "main chance" in order to state the facts.

Stock market critics endeavor to find a reason or explanation for the day's fluctuations. The price movement may be uniform—up or down—or it may be irregular, one stock or group of stocks advancing, others declining and others remaining dull and passive. He must search the field for the primary cause. At times this cause may be plain to everyone, again it may be concealed from the outsider's view and yet again the superficial factors may be written down as the cause when the true facts are completely hidden. The speculator can form his own conclusions regarding the merits of each critic by a study of the latter's work.

The criticism has been frequently made by speculators that nine out of ten newspapers are bullish at all times and through all markets. This is true, and the following story will partially explain why: The editor of a financial journal was a bear on the market. He believed in lower prices. He was committed to short contracts in the market and from day to day he gave his readers the benefit of his convictions, honestly and with enthusiasm. The market declined. Day by day, however, he lost subscribers, until finally the losses became too serious to be ignored. An important commission house among others notified him to discontinue its subscription of three copies. He first sent his business manager to the house in question for an explanation. A member of the firm said: "Your paper is bearish on the market. All our customers are bulls. Your paper is on file in our offices and our customers find a great deal of fault with it. It makes some of them very angry."

"But we have been right on the market?" "I can't help that; we can no longer ignore the complaints, for they are too numerous."

"If you continue to run a bear paper," reported the business manager to his editor, "you will ruin yourself."

The conclusion appears to be that the public will buy a newspaper that is bullish and wrong in its judgment, and desert a paper that is bearish and correct in its judgment.

The value of a newspaper writer's market views may depend to some extent on whether he is a speculator or an onlooker. Most newspaper writers speculate, although a minority do not. Undoubtedly the one who does not speculate is in a better position to advise than one who is prejudiced in favor of his own ventures just as the advice of the non-speculating broker is to be preferred to that of the speculator.

The field of prophecy is invaded to a greater or less extent by all financial critics. The more experienced the writer the less positive he will be in making predictions regarding price movements. It will also be observed by the speculator that the newspaper critic will carefully state two sides of a proposition and leave the reader in complete and illuminating possession of the fact that if "the market (or a special stock) does not go up it will go down." This is the easiest way out of a complicated situation and the reader can hardly dispute the accuracy of the conclusion.

Wall Street is served by two news bureaus with great energy. They print and distribute daily a mass of facts, figures, comment, prophecy and rumor. There are traders who find the compilation at times so confusing and contradictory that they ignore everything except definite new statements. Nevertheless, Wall Street would find it exceedingly difficult to get along without its news service, and it is a fact that each bureau strives with energy and intelligence to be accurate. At the conclusion of each day each bureau has a method of so analyzing the day's work that misstatements are accounted for by the reporters responsible.

The speculating student of the news bureau service should learn to differentiate between the varying statements. It is the desire of the bureau to print all rumors and gossip that it can gather and the relative values as market factors are very wide apart. For example, a statement made by the president of a bank of acknowledged authority is entitled to more consideration than an interview with "a leading banker." Then again a review of business conditions by a railroad officer under his name is more to be relied upon than the prophecies of a speculator along the same line. And to judge of the value of a statement regarding the copper, iron, or any other industry one must know something about the man, his reputation and his associates. Crop reports and opinions are notoriously misleading. Financial statements and statistical tables must be accepted with conservatism. The tendency is always to exaggeration rather than the opposite direction. The news bureaus do their work well and in this respect Wall Street ranks ahead of Lombard Street. If the speculator is to derive value from their service he must learn to classify the various items in the same spirit in which they are printed.

The genesis of a Wall Street rumor is a curious thing in itself. It is the function of the news bureau and the newspaper to print rumors whenever they appear to have foundation in fact. A rumor should always be verified before it is spread broadcast, but this sound rule of the newspaper is as often ignored as it is followed. Rumors are thickest regarding coming events which, according to the old adage, cast their shadows before.

For the purpose of illustration we will say that the Alphabet Mining Company is to have a dividend meeting on the 15th of the month. A change is to be made in the dividend as the company is doing a poor business. The rate of dividend had been 6 per cent per annum. It is reasonable to say that between the 10th and the 15th following will be some of the rumors:

1. The dividend will be passed.
2. The dividend will be reduced to 4 per cent.
3. A director says that the present dividend will be maintained as the situation is not as bad as represented.
4. The dividend will be reduced to 5 per cent.
5. The directors will postpone their meeting.

And so on others suggest themselves as even more commonplace. Or it may be a railroad meeting when it is intended to advance the rate of dividend and the company has been subjected to rumors of change of control. Prior to such a meeting the rumor maker is a very busy man.

Again, in times of panic, the writer has found it difficult to walk a few blocks in the Wall Street district without being stopped and "confidentially" informed that such and such a house is "in trouble." It is then that great mischief and injury can be accomplished by the newspaper writer, who must use tact and discretion in "killing" such rumors as they arise, for they are rarely based on facts. When failures occur, they are frequently unheralded and rarely preceded by rumors.

When private wires between New York, Boston and Chicago become commonplace the two latter cities become responsible for many Wall Street rumors. Chicago in particular seemed to keep a stereotyped line which read: "It is reported that ------ is dead." The blank space was filled in with the name of the President of the United States or that of any other person who would attract speedy attention. Boston's fancy ran to the creation of beautiful stories of mining, industrial and railroad deals. At times they have been worthy of an Indiana novelist for power of imagination and gift of expression.

The newspaper writer acquires the knack of almost knowing offhand the truth or falsity of a rumor. If it originates with a man who prefaces his statement with "I hear," "They say," "It is said," "A man I don't know says," or any other source of information equally unreliable, it is well to disbelieve the rumor. If a definite authority is named for the rumor, and it is not received at second or third hand, then you may have something worthy of investigation. A rumor is known by its father. A speculator should study the relative values of rumors and learn to take advantage of their market effects, always remembering that 90 per cent of them are not true, but that fiction as well as fact prevails in price making.

In conclusion, it can be said that the financial writer does not expect his reader to accept his views as final. It is not the function of the financial writer to win or lose money in speculation for the reader as so many small speculators believe. It is rather his duty to discuss as they arise those factors which govern the financial and economic situation, giving to each its proper place, and considering each with common sense, even temper and mature judgment.

The speculator will do well to remember that the financial writer has his own theories and prejudices; good, bad or indifferent judgment, and is only the doctor in so far as he endeavors to diagnose the case. He differs from the doctor in that he does not prescribe for the patient. Should he prescribe and become a prophet of prices, he is then like the doctor and also the lawyer in that he is not responsible for mistakes of judgment. The speculator pays the bill.

A writer in the *Wall Street Journal* discusses this question as follows:

A correspondent asks: "I notice that practically all the financial articles in the daily newspapers and most of the discussions of financial matters in other financial papers are always bullish in character. Why is this? I have been reading financial articles for many years, and, with very few exceptions, this has always been so. Can you explain it?"

In order to understand what is involved in the answer to the above query, it is necessary to have a clear idea of what a "bull" is. A bull is a man who has something to sell and is desirous of selling it at a good price. Consequently he is anxious for prices to go up in order that he may sell. A bear, on the contrary, is a man who wishes to buy at a low price.

Now, the end and object of all Wall Street finance is just one thing, namely, the gathering up of public money in exchange for securities distributed to the public. A Wall Street banker in active business is engaged in a process that may be called the manufacture and sale of securities. Much the largest part of his work consists in turning securities into cash, either for his own account or for the account of other bankers, in return for a commission. There are times when the financial community needs the public's money less than at other times, but, taking it all in all, anything that tends to whet the public's appetite for securities so that it is in a mood to exchange its cash for securities is satisfactory to what are commonly called the large financial interests.

Consequently these large financial interests are always, or almost always, concerned in keeping the public in proper disposition toward the security market. They are always anxious to prevent the public from becoming alarmed, and they are usually willing to assist in stimulating the public's speculative desires.

This is probably one reason why the published articles in the daily papers are so generally optimistic in character alike through good and bad times. It has become a maxim in Wall Street that the public, or, rather, Wall Street, will endure any amount of inaccuracy, and even misrepresentation, as long as its effect is bullish at least for the time being.

The public does not realize, and probably never will realize, that it is the court of last resort in all important financial operations. It is its custom to regard itself as helpless, at the mercy of shrewd financiers and unscrupulous speculators. If it could only once get it into its head that it holds the key to the situation in its own hands and that without its money the large financial interests could of themselves do little or nothing, and if, in addition to this, it would take a little pains to inform itself as to actual facts, figures and values, very much less money would be lost in Wall Street and a great many enterprises would never be undertaken. Stocks and bonds are never sold until they are sold to the public. Manipulators may move prices up and down on the Exchange and may make fictitious transactions to an enormous extent, but unless the public comes with its money and buys the securities, the work is unavailing.

Of course, it is not fair to suggest that the generally bullish character of financial comment at all times is the result of prearranged plans in behalf of the large financial interests as against the public. The hopeful and even the optimistic side of things is necessarily the more popular of the two sides. Moreover, as a rule, the conditions that make for higher prices of securities are conditions favorable to the business world and to the public. Consequently it is pleasanter to look at the cheerful side of things than at the other side. Nevertheless, it is perhaps true to say that, on the whole, there is somewhat too much of this kind of thing and too little of its opposite. Only too often it has happened that the public has been pretty generally encouraged up to the last minute, and when trouble has come and the public's money has been lost, the only consolation that it gets is usually in the form of a mild scolding for not having foreseen the trouble before it came.

A healthy skepticism is seldom out of place in Wall Street, so far as speculation is concerned. Money is very seldom lost thereby. People who have had experience covering one or two panics know very well that the first lesson that has to be learned by the successful speculator is the avoidance of the disaster always caused by a panic. The very essence of a panic is that it sweeps away every one who is overtrading—whether it be to a large or to a small extent. Of what use is it to pile up imposing paper profits if they are all to be swept away when the tidal wave strikes? The only way whereby people can avoid being caught in a panic is by the exercise at all times of great conservatism and considerable skepticism. The successful speculator must be content at times to ignore probably two out of every three apparent opportunities to make money, and must know how to sell and take his profits when the "bull" chorus is loudest. When he has learned that much, he has learned a great deal.

CHAPTER XXI.

The Physical Position of the Stock Speculator.

I t is a habit with some active speculators to attribute their own lack of success to advantages of physical position; that is to say, the outside trader believes that the member of the Exchange is in a relatively more advantageous position to make money. The broker is "on the spot," and is in such close relationship to the market that he commands greater opportunities and less risk than the outsider, according to the latter's conclusion, which is not always true. As a fact, however, they occupy distinctly different positions and employ radically different methods, although having the same object, viz., money making.

It is reasonable to hold that the member of the Exchange who trades for his own account, occupies a relationship to the market which gives him substantial advantages—independent of commissions—as compared with his position were he an outside trader, located in New York, Chicago or elsewhere.

As an illustration we can use the case of a young Chicago Hebrew, who graduated from Harvard, and who selected stock trading as a vocation. His father, a successful trader, was in complete sympathy with his ambition. The young man started to trade in the New York Stock Exchange market over a Chicago wire. He lost money. He figured that as a trader he was handicapped by certain conditions which he could eliminate. His view was that he lost several minutes in the transmission of the quotations from the floor of the Exchange over the ticker, more time in the transmission of the quotations from New York to Chicago, additional time in their distribution throughout that city and fresh delay in the transmission of his order to New York, thence to the Exchange, and in its execution. Although the machinery required in the processes enumerated has been perfected in a high degree and narrowed down to seconds, the trader who sought to make "quick turns" undoubtedly clearly comprehended the disadvantages or handicaps under which he labored.

He therefore left Chicago for New York, and traded from the office of a Stock Exchange house, alternately watching and studying the ticker or the blackboard quotations as his fancy dictated. The real or imagined advantages did not result in substantial profits and after a fair trial of trading from the outside he bought a Stock Exchange membership and became a daily trader. He was now free to roam as he pleased, study the habits and methods of individual brokers and groups of brokers in the execution of orders, the tricks of the trade, the relative value of gossip designed to make fluctuations. His early speculations were by no means entirely successful; parental assistance being required to help the young trader carry a block of stock with which he became entangled in a brief period of great mental excitement.

At the expiration of a year, however, the trader had become a practical money maker who derived his livelihood from daily hazards in the stock market. He is, as might be expected, of the opinion that as an active trader he is free from disadvantages with which the outsider has to contend.

But it may be held that not all traders may become members of the Stock Exchange and that to become a "trader-broker" requires qualities of temperament not always to be found in successful speculators who are not Exchange members. And the outsider may hold that, given capable brokers, a quiet office, a ticker and the news of the day, and his advantages will more than offset those of the Exchange member. In the first place he will prefer a quiet office to the babble of voices and confusion of the Exchange floor. Absolute quiet may be to him a foremost consideration. Secondly, he sits alongside the ticker from which position he can study purchases and sales, supply and demand and market tones, factors that call for careful study by the professional trader. The time lost in the execution of his order he regards as more than offset by the condition which enables him to calmly read the tape and draw rapid conclusions as to the significance of the transactions so quickly printed.

Yet another consideration is that which comes from trading in an office receiving good market gossip, calculated to influence prices. Thus one office may possess very substantial advantages over another. It may be represented on the floor by brokers clever enough to keep the office informed of the Board Room gossip and news; it may possess superior sources of news information, such as newspaper financial writers occupying desk room therein or close relationship with this or that powerful speculative or banking faction or clique. The successful outside trader knows that market activity on his part must be accompanied by quick decision, the possession of correct market judgment and the entire day at his disposal.

Men rather than markets differ. The experience of traders suggests the conclusion that as each trader has a different temperament, arriving at conclusions from entirely different points of view, and calling for different conditions, each position (1) trading on the Exchange floor and (2) trading from a New York office in a favorable environment has advantages and disadvantages which almost balance.

In this consideration of the questions involved the point of view prevails that each of the two brokers is an Exchange member. One executes his own orders, after which it costs him $1.12 to clear each 100 shares of stock, while the other entrusts the execution to another member and the net cost is $3.12 per 100 shares. The floor trader, therefore, has a $2 advantage on each 100 share trade. Should the outside trader not be a member of the Exchange his commission bills will place him in this position: The board member holds a $75,000 membership. Money is, say, worth 5 per cent and therefore his initial expense is $3,750 per annum. To be even with the game he must net that sum in any one year, plus his clearance bills. The outsider starts without any fixed charge of this character. Should, however, the outsider be a very active or heavy trader his commission bills would soon exceed the expenses of the Exchange member. The average trader, however, does not pay $3,750 a year in commissions. This question of expense is one to be determined by the individual trader, who should have no difficulty in arriving at the proper course to pursue.

To compare the number of successful outside traders with the number of successful Exchange member traders does not lead to accurate conclusions. The number of traders in the 1,100 membership of the Stock Exchange is of necessity limited, and the number of outside traders is many times greater, consequently the outsiders can point to superior numbers. But in comparing the accounts of 25 members and 25 outside traders the figures would favor the members.

Consideration of the questions involved will lead to the conclusion that the outside daily trader, dealing from a branch office in New York or in another city, is at a round disadvantage as compared with the floor-trading member or the office-trading member.

The experience of Wall Street men, legitimate brokers and bucket shop proprietors, is that the outside daily trader (not an Exchange member) is rarely successful. He is reduced to the position of a bettor, heavily handicapped, and obliged to pay a fee of $25 on each guess, plus the interest on his account. It must be conceded, however, that the chances of failure of the occasional trader, who deals from a distance, are obviously not so great as those of the trader making daily ventures. Where the latter is almost absolutely certain to fail in the long run, the occasional trader occupies a very much safer position.

CHAPTER XXII.

TEMPERAMENT AND EQUIPMENT.

The man of phlegmatic temperament, who can lose without feeling mental depression and who can win without corresponding elation, is the man who is best adapted for speculation, provided he possesses the other necessary qualifications. It should not be understood, however, that the nervous temperament is not represented by many successful speculators; in fact the majority of speculators are very nervous men. Many of them are troubled with nervous diseases. The most successful stock speculators of the day are sufferers from nervous indigestion, attributable to worry and irregular habits in eating and drinking during periods of active speculation. There are speculators who are unable to eat during the Stock Exchange session; others can digest only the lightest and most digestible foods; others smoke and drink freely and do not eat, and still others, win or lose, eat heartily with unimpaired digestive organs. The advantage is naturally with the latter group, for such a temperament, with regular habits, makes far stronger vitality than is possessed by the extremely nervous man. A sound body makes a sound mind, and good health is a factor of importance with the speculator. One of the cleverest of the younger speculators on the Stock Exchange inherited his membership from his father, also a successful speculator, and who died of a nervous disease which was in all probability attributable to the uncertainty of his trade. The son, who is essentially a moneymaker, rivaling his father, suffers from nervousness to a greater degree than his father, and at frequent intervals is obliged to leave Wall Street and travel for rest and recreation.

An unknown writer, considering the qualities essential to the equipment of a speculator, names them in this order: (1) self-reliance; (2) judgment; (3) courage; (4) prudence; (5) pliability.

1. *Self-reliance.* A man must think for himself; must follow his own convictions. George Macdonald says: 'A man cannot have another man's ideas any more than he can have another man's soul or another man's body.' Self-trust is the foundation of successful effort.

2. *Judgment.* That equipoise, that nice adjustment of the faculties one to the other which is called good judgment, is an essential to the speculator.

3. *Courage.* That is, confidence to act on the decisions of the mind. In speculation there is value in Mirabeau's dictum: 'Be bold, still be bold, always be bold.'

4. *Prudence.* The power of measuring the danger, together with a certain alertness and watchfulness, is very important. There should be a balance of these two, prudence and courage; prudence in contemplation, courage in execution. Lord Bacon says: 'In meditation all dangers should be seen; in execution none, unless very formidable.' Connected with these qualities, properly an outgrowth of them, is a third, viz., promptness. The mind convinced, the act should follow. In the words of Macbeth: 'Henceforth the very firstlings of my heart shall be the firstlings of my hand.' Think, act, promptly.

5. *Pliability.* The ability to change an opinion, the power of revision. 'He who observes,' says Emerson 'and observes again, is always formidable.'

"The qualifications named are necessary to the make-up of a speculator, but they must be in well-balanced combination.

A deficiency or an overplus of one quality will destroy the effectiveness of all. The possession of such faculties in a proper adjustment is, of course, uncommon. In speculation, as in life, few succeed; many fail."

CHAPTER XXIII.

THE BROKER AND HIS CLIENT.

There are two classes of brokers dealing with the public: (1) the speculating stock broker, and (2) the non-speculating stock broker.

Preferably, the broker who does not speculate is to be employed. He occupies an unprejudiced position toward the market, and his opinion is therefore more valuable than that of the broker who is a speculator, and is swayed this way and that by every turn in the market. What is more natural than that he should advise his customer to trade as he is trading in the conviction that his judgment is right and in the belief that the customer's trade will help his own?

A physician will not prescribe for himself or his family treatment that he will successfully prescribe for others. Some brokers acknowledge, without hesitation, that while they can successfully advise and conduct the market operations of other persons they are dismal failures in conducting ventures for their own account. Many firms of brokers—and they are to be preferred in the selection of a broker—on signing articles of co-partnership stipulate that no firm member shall be permitted to speculate. Experience has taught them that in this way only are the risks of the stock commission trade minimized. Large operators select houses of this class for the execution of manipulative orders whenever it is possible to do so. By so doing they increase the margin of safety from the points of view of non-interference and financial stability.

There are traders who believe that the chances of success are increased when they trade with a firm which is identified with the operations of a leading manipulator. At times doubtless this selection is to be commended, provided the trader always remembers that his interests are distinctly a secondary consideration and that in an emergency the operator in question will protect himself even at the expense of the customers.

A trader in stocks should, when possible, make a study of his broker. He will find that brokers vary as much in mental habit and conscience as they do in appearance. There are brokers who will ascertain what their customers are desirous of doing in the market and advise them accordingly. The writer on more than one occasion has heard brokers offer advice that was absolutely contradictory in the effort to influence trading. For example: A was advised to buy a certain stock, having expressed belief in the view that it would advance, while B, ten minutes later was advised to sell the same stock short, having informed his broker that he believed in a decline. The singular result was that both customers lost money, each trader closing out at a loss on the minor fluctuations. The broker encouraged "trading" and profited by his commissions. There are brokers who will strain their consciences to the point of spraining to encourage trading, but they should not be difficult to detect.

In opening an account the reputation of a broker should carry weight. Is he an old or a new hand? Has he been successful? Are his customers of the permanent or transient class? Does he advise frequent or occasional ventures?

The exigencies of his trade require that the broker should preserve an impassive demeanor. He must not be disturbed by his clients' losses. If he were thus swayed by sentiment he would be in as dangerous a position as the too sympathetic nurse at the bedside of a precariously sick patient. The broker is navigating a craft that calls for a cool head at all times, especially in times of panic. If he were to sympathize with every client who loses, he would soon be a nervous wreck, retire from business or find an exhausted bank account. A successful broker of twenty years' experience has on his books small accounts aggregating $100,000, which he made good with his personal check. "I doubt," said he, in discussing the subject, "that I would pay those losses had I to do it again. The men were ungrateful in almost every instance. As a practice to be followed in trade I have no hesitation in condemning it. It is bad for the broker and bad for his client."

The honest and capable broker wants to have his client make money. A successful following is the best advertisement a broker can have. He will try to advise his clients so that they will make money. His advisory attitude to his client will be determined by the mental and financial capabilities of his client and the latter's attitude to the market and particular stocks.

CHAPTER XXIV.

THE BUCKET SHOP.

A bucket shop is a place where bets can be made on the advance or decline of stocks. The bettor deposits his margin, which may be 1 to 10 per cent, and "buys" or "sells" a specified stock. The dealer accepts the margin and nominally "buys" or "sells" the stock in question. There is no actual sale or purchase, as the dealer simply "buckets" the order, which is to say, that he agrees to pay any losses that he may sustain should his customer make a winning wager, and on the other hand if the customer loses, the dealer or bucket shop operator, profits by the exact amount of the bettor's loss.

The theory of the bucket shop operator is that four speculators out of five, and even a greater percentage, lose money in the long run if they become steady traders. They aim to obtain the money thus lost, and are willing to back their belief that the stock market is "unbeatable," by the average speculator.

Bucket shops have been engaged in business for more than twenty-five years. Many unsuccessful attempts have been made to suppress them. Since their early days the bucket shop system has expanded to tremendous limits; in the aggregate a large sum of money is invested in the trade, and the statement that millions of dollars are annually lost and won in this form of stock gambling is moderate and conservative. Twenty years ago the only important bucket shop in Wall Street and New York was that of Louis Todd, a New England man, who conducted a large establishment at 44 Broad, which extended through to and had an entrance on New Street. Hundreds of impecunious, broken down speculators and clerks gambled there, and Todd, the backer of the game, waxed fat and rich, building two Broadway hotels—the Marlborough and Vendome—on part of his profits. When he became a millionaire he retired from business. In the meantime, dozens of little bucket shops sprung up in lower New Street, until certain buildings in that neighborhood were regarded as little better than pest holes by the Wall Street community. Those bucket shops were conducted by cheap gamblers who, after running a week, would fail, the proprietor closing the doors and absconding with the money, while the "customers" were out the amount of their ventures. In a week or two the defaulting bucket shop operator would have no hesitation in resuming business in another office under another name. There may have been occasional honest failures, where the bank account was legitimately lost to the concern's bettors, but they were very few. Except at rare intervals those engaged in this trade have never been disturbed. Dishonest failures are so frequent that it seems strange that the criminal law is not more actively engaged in punishing those so plainly employed in this form of robbery.

Since 1890 the bucket shop system has advanced to such an extent that it now plays a very important part in the trade of stock speculation. It has been perfected so that many speculators are unable to distinguish the legitimate from the illegitimate firm and is now closely interwoven with stock speculation wherever it exists. There are bucket shops of the following types:

1. One which caters to a local trade on a limited capital.
2. One which poses as a banking firm, advertising extensively, has no Exchange memberships, and seeks a local mail order and private wire trade with the large cities.
3. One which operates and holds an Exchange membership.

4. One which operates a private wire system, but has no local trade, and depends for profits on the losses of country town investors.
5. An outwardly respectable firm which buckets its trade when necessity arises.

The bucket shop represented by the first type is conducted by men of no responsibility. It will open with a cash capital of $100, $1,000 or nothing at all if the operator is desperate. It will remain open just so long as bettors lose money to it, for the operators rarely remain long enough to pay out all the margins that have been deposited. The favorite lot traded in is one of 5 shares, while ten share trades are the limit. Margins of 1 per cent are required and 2 per cent is usually the limit. The commission is ⅛ or ¼. When margins are about to be exhausted, the bettor can remargin his venture if he so elects.

From 1896 to 1902, owing to the advancing market, there were many large failures of bucket shops transacting business in the group designated as type No. 2. There are many in operation to-day, and in the number there are several which are very strong financially. Their customers are pleased with their methods and are unable to distinguish them from legitimate firms. They maintain elaborate offices, spend thousands of dollars in advertising and disseminate expensive books and pamphlets to prospective losers.

In group 3 are found bucket shops which consider that an Exchange membership cloak is a valuable asset in obtaining business. They are the concerns which "match orders" on an exchange and consider themselves to be somewhat better than their competitors.

The private wire bucket shop has a central office in Wall Street. It leases a system of private wires, transmits quotations and employs agents on a profit sharing or salary basis. Usually the identity of the owner or backers is concealed under such a title, as for example, The New York Stock Commission Co. At times they employ as many as a dozen telegraph operators and deal not only in stocks, but also in grain and cotton. Members of this group are believed to have conducted highly profitable operations. Their customers are inexperienced, and the out-of-town speculator is regarded in this trade as a swift loser.

Those included in group 5 will resent the indignity, as they can hardly be classed as bucket shops, although resorting to bucket shop methods when the financial sky threatens disaster. Firms in this class are Exchange members. The members of such a firm may be carrying a large line of stocks. A decline is inevitable. The firm requests its customers to liquidate and the advice is unheeded; on the contrary the speculators may insist on buying more stocks. In order to escape the fury of the storm, the firm decides to jettison part of the cargo, and so with self-preservation in view, rather than assume further risks, the firm sells part or all of its customers' line of stocks, and stands in the position of having "bucketed" its customers' accounts. As soon, however, as the storm has passed, they are rebought. The brokers, it is true, have profited by their customers' losses. All the rules governing Exchange trading are complied within this operation, for when the stocks were sold, they were sold for the individual account of one of the members of the firm and stand as a short sale, for which he or the firm is responsible on the books. Money made is credited to this account just as money lost is debited. The broker simply wagers that his customers will lose, and rather than jeopardize his own position, he pursues this course. When you read that a brokerage concern has failed because its customers did not respond to "margin calls," you will know that the suspended firm succumbed to the conditions which the "bucketing" broker wished to avoid when he sold his customers' stocks.

The bucket shop appeals to several speculators, notably

1. The small trader whose account is refused by legitimate concerns;
2. The trader who believes that he can more advantageously trade on board quotations than on open market quotations; and
3. The trader who deals in a bucket shop rather than in the New York market by mail or telegraph order.

The small speculators supply the bulk of the bucket shop profits. Speculators of the second class are in error for the dealer overcomes his seeming advantage with tricks peculiar to the trade. Those in group 3 would be richer in pocket if they refrained absolutely from trading.

Some of the theories and views of bucket shop operators are:

That $5,000 is sufficient capital with which to open for business.

That four out of five speculators lose money in stock speculation and that the steady player is sure to lose.

That the most certain losers are the small speculators, and those who operate on a margin.

That the smaller the margin the greater the chance of loss by the speculator, hence the preference for small margins.

That to encourage a speculator to pyramid on his success and enlarge the scope of his transactions is to win all his money in the long run.

That it is policy to pay out winnings promptly to new customers, who once satisfied of financial responsibility are forever after credulous.

That speculators rarely draw down their profits, but persist invariably in wanting more, and in this fact exists the bucket shop operators' safety.

"Of course," explained a bucket shop broker to the writer, "this is a gambling game. There are thousands of tricks to it. The average speculator is a fool in believing that he can guess a game which he knows nothing about. For example, suppose a large bucket shop has persuaded its customers to buy in the aggregate 10,000 shares of Sugar on small margins. It is short just that much on the books. The operator will then make a play in the open market. He will send in a broker he employs to the Sugar crowd, and there are times when he has his own representative on the Exchange, to sell the market off a couple of points in order to wipe out his customers' accounts. He is willing to lose $1,000 to make $10,000. This has been done many times. And then again, I have known clever adventurers to work precisely the same game with the bucket shops. They have planted orders in all the bucket shops and then have hastily manipulated the stock market to successfully execute a heavy winning play.

"When Gov. Flower died in 1899, there was hardly a solvent bucket shop in the country. They had paid out all their own capital, and all their customers' margins, and millions more were liabilities on their books. Had their customers made a concerted demand for their money, not one could have kept its doors open. The smash came and in one day every bucket shop account was wiped out; the operators had all the money, and they started afresh without a liability.

"In conducting a large bucket shop, it is almost impossible to make a big winning on a bull market such as the one of recent years. Almost all bucket shop traders are bulls. In a rapidly shifting two-sided market with broad fluctuations, the bucket shop will always reap a harvest. The bucket shop has no use for customers who trade and take small losses and attempt to scalp the market. They want speculators who will 'guess' the market for 'big money,' the fellows who 'buy 'em when they are strong and sell 'em when they are weak.'

100

"There are concerns engaged in the business of bucketing trade who have never been suspected of such a thing and so elaborate are their precautions that they will never be suspected. With an abundance of capital and knowledge of the business, a bucket shop operator knows that he stands behind one of the best money-making gambling institutions in the country.

"When a bucket shop secures an undesirable customer— one who can make money—it will try to freeze him out. A few years ago $5,000 was regarded as a fair amount of cash with which to embark in this trade. To-day the amount required is larger. A bucket shop starting with $100,000 will pay out to its backers as dividends the first $100,000 that comes in the office and trust to luck to continue in business on the margins of its customers. Should this plan 'go wrong,' the custom is to assess the backers of the game, and if an assessment plan is rejected by them, the bucket shop suspends or 'welches' as you please to call it. One of the singular things about the bucket shop speculators is that as a class they will return and do business with a concern which has failed and resumed.

"Experience teaches a bucket shop operator that the average speculator will play the game in this way: He is a bull and buys stocks. He is successful and runs $100 into $1,000. He then writes for, or demands in person, his principal and profits. The money is promptly paid. The successful speculator then concludes that the firm is financially sound. He believes that he is the one man in 1,000 who can call the turns of the market. Fortune is in his grasp. Success makes him conceited, less careful and more daring. He returns the $1,000 and possibly more. He may interest one or two friends to try the same rapid road to fortune. He resumes trading on the bull side.

"Giving him the best luck possible, we find that he has increased his $1,000 to $2,000. The chances are that he is now overtrading, or scattered all over the board—trading in too many stocks—and so extended that any sharp set back in the market will wipe him out. Along comes an unfavorable development. The market breaks 1, 2, 3, 4 or 5 points and our speculating country customer is wiped out.

"The lesson does not prove to be a valuable one. The speculator tries again. He has abandoned his idea that he is going to make a fortune. He now humbly aspires to "get even," or in other words, to recover his lost money. In the attempt to "get even," he loses more money and then sensibly quits gambling in stocks or becomes a confirmed 'piker' and a victim of the gambling habit. Once acquired by a poor man, it is as hard to shake off as a taste for strong drink. It will pauperize him and make it almost impossible for him to take up genuine work and become a useful citizen in the community."

The bucket shop speculator injures his own chances of success the very minute that he gives an order. Supply and demand are the basic factors influencing the price of stocks. When demand exceeds supply, prices advance and opposite conditions result in declines. The bucket shop purchase is shorn of power to influence prices, for the order has not been executed in the open market. Assuming that 50,000 shares of stocks are bought in the bucket shops of the United States in a single day—and the estimate is conservative—it will be observed that this buying power is absolutely a negative factor in influencing enhancement of stock values which would mean profit to the speculative buyers. On the other hand, such a buying demand, with the orders actually executed on the floor of the Stock Exchange, would at times stimulate an advance, check a decline or exert an otherwise important influence. It will therefore be perceived that the bucket shop speculator is a force arrayed against himself; that he enters the game with many handicaps and penalizes himself by reducing his venture to a wholly negative value as a price maker.

It has been argued that precisely the same conditions prevail with orders executed on the Consolidated Exchange, but this is an erroneous view, for in all such transactions the actual delivery of stock balances is contemplated and made. Where there remains at the expiration of any day or week a balance to be received or delivered in stocks, and the stocks are not available on the Consolidated Exchange, then its brokers resort to the primary market—the Stock Exchange—and purchase any stocks that may be required to balance their accounts, or sell if the circumstances call for sales.

The writer has heard occasionally of individuals who have made winnings in bucket shops. He has never heard of any man who became rich as a bucket shop speculator or even had the common sense to take down substantial winnings and retire from the contest. While conceding that there are times when the purchase or sale of stocks, even in a bucket shop, results in profit to the speculator, an examination of bucket shop accounts shows conclusively that in the long run the bucket shop speculator is certain to become bankrupt; while they are also suggestive of the belief that the average bucket shop speculator fails to understand the first principles of the game.

A contemporary writer says: "The large number of gambling places in the country known as bucket shops, with their frequent failures and resultant disclosure of their unscrupulous methods, yet with a train of victims which seemingly is larger after each new exposure, is causing a great deal of moralizing these days, provoking troubled inquiry whether the American people are more foolish and ignorant than they are usually thought to be, and whether this folly and ignorance is growing.

"There is no doubt that among the customers of these bucket shops there are many of the gullible sort who spend their lives and what little cash resources they possess in attempting to extract wealth from one visionary project after another. But the fundamental reason why bucket shops flourish is that the American people as a people are irresistibly fond of financial speculation. While our countrymen can in no ways be called a nation of gamblers, and while great speculative manias, such as the South Sea bubble, the John Law scheme, or the tulip craze have never possessed the whole country, as each in turn swept over parts of Europe in the last two centuries, there exists a strong element in our national character wherein the love of venture and the dominance of a lively imagination hold full sway. This tendency, of course, is most noticeable in a period of great prosperity like that which so happily exists at present; and the most natural direction of this manifestation is in the shares of the great railway and industrial corporations through which the country's prosperity chiefly pulsates.

"The bucket shop offers the readiest road of speculation. The man in a country village who would hesitate to put $10 upon a roulette wheel would willingly buy ten shares of a railway stock in the office of one of the numerous 'investment companies' or bucket shops of similar high names which are located in his town. Stock speculation through the regular channels of a Stock Exchange house is costly and complicated. The commissions and interest charges are large and most of these houses do not care to accept small amounts or to deal in less than one hundred shares of stock, save for very well-known customers. It is carried on with difficulty by a speculator living in a small town where he does not have frequent access to market reports. And the customer of a Stock Exchange house may, if the market goes heavily against him, lose not only the margin of his investment, but find himself heavily in debt to his broker besides.

"Bucket shops do business on a very different principle. They neither buy nor sell the stocks upon orders given to them by their customers, and in very many instances they make no pretence of assuming to do this, nor do their customers have any idea that their "orders" to buy and sell are obeyed. Both parties to the operation look upon it in its true light of a simple bet made that a stock quoted upon the New York Exchange will go up or down within certain limits. The commission charged by the bucket shop keeper is much less than that of a Stock Exchange firm. The bucket shop man is willing to deal in very small lots of stock, accepting very small margins. He charges his customer no interest for the money which, if the business was done in the usual way, would have to be borrowed to pay for the stocks actually purchased. Moreover, the bucket shop keeper allows his customer to begin or close his trade at a definitive quotation as it appears upon the ticker of the Stock Exchange operations, and he closes the customer's account instantly upon the exhaustion of the margin, so that the customer is assured that no further claim is to be made upon him in case the market still continues to go against him. The bucket shop keeper however, for his part, often declines to allow an accumulated profit in certain stocks to run beyond a certain figure and he generally is willing to deal in but small lots of stock. His whole system of doing business is one which presents very great inducements to the small speculator, and if these inducements could be offered by any responsible house having a membership in the Stock Exchange, that house would very soon have a monopoly of speculative operations conducted by the outside public in Wall Street. "Where, then, does the bucket shop keeper make his money? In this simply, that, as his operations are, in reality, those of a series of bets with his customers, the bets, so far as the customers are concerned, taking the form of guesses as to which way the stock market will go, experience has demonstrated that such guesses of the general run of people are in the main incorrect and that there is a steady, average profit to be had in miscellaneously accepting, or as the slang of Wall Street has it, 'coppering' them. As most of the outsiders are 'lambs,' as they are called in Wall Street, they buy stocks, rather than sell them, so that the customers of bucket shops find their greatest profit and the keeper of the concern his greatest loss, in periods of prosperity and advancing markets such as we have just seen. Then if the bucket shop man is a dishonest individual, as he usually is, he finds it convenient to fail at the proper time, sweeping into his own pockets all the margins and paper profits of his patrons. Many of these patrons, indeed, are very far from being innocent and unsuspecting lambs. They have no illusions on the score of the game they are playing, and they know that the bucket shop keeper is probably a pretty 'crooked' person. They are apt to belong to that unhappy class of individuals known as the 'ghosts' of Wall Street, that is, men who once did business there on a large scale, but have lost the money they won and are forced to gamble, if they gamble at all in a very humble way. The question, on which these men concentrate most of their attention is the possibility of the bucket shop failing, and after a prolonged Trail market when they know that the proprietor of the concern is probably losing heavily, they take their profits in cash, if they have any, and beware the shop as a very dangerous locality.

"It is very clear, therefore, that the business of trying to speculate by means of bucket shops is an extremely hazardous thing. If man feels he must speculate, he ought to become a customer of a house having membership in the Stock or Consolidated Exchanges. And it is still as true as it ever was that the best way to make money is not to speculate at all."

CHAPTER XXV.

The Speculator and the Consolidated Exchange.

The speculator should have a clear idea of the Consolidated Exchange, its advantages and disadvantages and relation to the Stock Exchange. This is necessary inasmuch as the Consolidated Exchange has at times afforded a market for many thousand small speculators in stocks, particularly those living out of town. The Consolidated Exchange is generally advertised as the "N. Y. Con. Stock Exchange." It is a consolidation of a mining exchange and an oil exchange. In the '70's and '80's it was the scene of violent speculation in mining stocks, and certificates representing crude oil in lots of 1,000 barrels. Accompanying the decline of speculation in mining shares and oil certificates, the members decided to trade in the active stocks dealt in on the Stock Exchange. To-day the trading in mining shares is on a nominal basis only, while the pipe line certificate as a speculative factor has been entirely eliminated, hence the name New York Consolidated Stock and Petroleum Exchange is a misnomer, and the substitution of the assumed title—"N. Y. Con. Stock Exchange." Almost the entire floor of the Consolidated Exchange is now devoted to dealing in Stock Exchange shares. In the main, the dealings are confined to fractured lots; in fact the bulk of the trading is in 10 share lots. Certain members of the Consolidated Exchange are accustomed to say that their Board is the "primary market" for speculation in fractional lots. This is not so. The Stock Exchange is the primary market for the sale of each and every stock dealt in thereon. On its quotations, questions before courts of law are decided and its prices are recognized as official in any legal dispute involving the price of 1 share or its multiple. Then again, inasmuch, as it is impossible to deal on the Consolidated Exchange in many inactive stocks listed on the Stock Exchange, the limitations of such a market obviously make the claim to a "primary market" absurd. And again, it is possible to conceive of the complete elimination of the Consolidated Exchange, without thereby affecting investors, speculators, or those corporate interests which have listed their securities on the Stock Exchange after compliance with the rules of the latter institution.

Whether the Consolidated Exchange is or is not a useful public institution are questions which will not be answered here. Membership on the Consolidated Exchange is nominally quoted at $2,500. Stock Exchange memberships (in 1902) commanded $83,000. The disparity in values is also calculated to cheapen the "primary market" claim. In connection with the Consolidated Exchange there have been many scandalous failures in which credulous investors have in the aggregate been robbed of a large amount of money. Bucket shops have secured representation in the institution, and the later-day management has not yet been able to overcome the corruption which was fostered in the early '90's.

Of all Consolidated Exchange assets and possessions figuratively the most valuable is the "black-board." This "black-board" is the largest in the country. Its length is almost that of a city block. Two men are employed from 10 A. M. to 3 P. M. to post thereon the quotations received by a telegraph operator who calls them off as rapidly as they are received. Where the quotations come from no one knows, as the Stock Exchange does not recognize the Consolidated Exchange and would not permit it to use the official prices if any means could be devised to exclusively hold them. It is reasonable to believe, however, that the Consolidated Exchange has at some remote point secured a Stock Exchange ticker or connection with a telegraph wire on which Stock Exchange quotations are transmitted. There are two stock quotation telegraph companies. One supplies tickers transmitting quotations to Stock Exchange members exclusively. That is the fastest ticker service. The other, and slower ticker, by perhaps one or two minutes, can be obtained by Consolidated Exchange firms, hotels and public places generally, provided two members of the Stock Exchange will indorse the application of the person who wishes to rent one or more. On the floor of the Consolidated Exchange there are two of the slower tickers separated from and apart from the blackboard. Many efforts have been made by the Stock Exchange to have those tickers removed, but in the legal contests resulting from such attempts the Consolidated Exchange has successfully maintained its right to possession and use. How the two tickers on the Consolidated Exchange floor are used by the members will hereafter be explained. The Consolidated Exchange has a small ticker service of its own, but to it no particular importance is attached. Now Stock Exchange quotations are also received by Consolidated Exchange members in one other way, although this fact is not generally known, and certainly not by the public. It requires no explanation to understand that inasmuch as the Consolidated Exchange must rely on its two slow tickers on its floor, and its posted blackboard quotations which are slower than the ticker (because they are probably transmitted from a similar ticker) that the speculator who can get Stock Exchange prices through the medium of the fast ticker or by telephone from the floor of the Stock Exchange can trade at a substantial advantage over his competitors. Taking advantage of his "quick" prices he can, when there is a broad market, undersell or outbid his fellow members by ⅛'s, ¼'s or even full points, provided they are dependent on the slower quotation facilities.

Trading on the Consolidated Exchange is conducted by the following dealers:

1. The legitimate commission firm which executes and closes out its customers' transactions without departing from the recognized rules.
2. The illegitimate commission firm, which is in fact a bucket shop, and which evades the rules.
3. The speculator who trades for his own account to save commissions and expenses that trading through a Stock Exchange house would necessitate.
4. The room-trader who scalps fractions and "evens up" his business at the end of each session.
5. The trader who relies upon quick quotation service in order to make profitable ventures.
6. The arbitrage trader who trades between the New York, Philadelphia and Boston markets.
7. The broker who executes orders for other brokers. Total membership in the Consolidated Exchange is limited to 2,400 and about one-fifth of that number are active members.

Legitimate commission firms are not few and transact a very respectable volume of business. Their customers, as a rule, are 10-share traders, although many firms have customers who deal in 100 share lots and more. Up to 1902 the commission charged for a fractional share trade—50 shares or under—was 1-16 of 1 per cent or one half the Stock Exchange commission, but the rate was increased by vote of members to ⅛ of 1 per cent, thus placing the two Boards on a parity; but on lots of 50 shares or more the charge is 1-6 of 1 per cent each way or ⅛ of 1 per cent for the round transaction. In the three or four most active stocks on the Consolidated Exchange the commission broker contends that he can always give his customer the Stock Exchange price or one approximating it ⅛ or ¼ per cent. On the other hand, he holds that the fractional lot trader—as distinguished from the 100 share trader—is at a disadvantage on the Stock Exchange inasmuch as custom compels him to accept or pay ¼, ½, ¾, 1 per cent or even more on 10 shares as it is offered or bought. There are also times when he can give his customer the advantage of fractions, as during an excited rising market the Consolidated Exchange prices will rise faster than those on the Stock Exchange, but it is obvious that in such an instance that which works to the advantage of the seller must be the disadvantage of the buyer, while the proposition is exactly reversed if the speculation is for the decline, as distinguished from the rise. The Consolidated Exchange member will at times when he does not find a broad market execute large orders on the Stock Exchange paying the regular commission of ⅛. This latter fact proves that his own market has clearly defined limitations as distinguished from the primary market, and also that he has telephonic—almost instantaneous—connection with the floor of the Stock Exchange. The following conclusions regarding the facilities of the Consolidated Exchange commission firm which executes its orders are fair:

1. The market for fractional lots in the favorite and most active speculative stocks is an excellent one and a trader in 10 share certificates can usually buy and sell closer to Stock Exchange 100 share lot prices than he can on the Stock Exchange itself.

2. The market for large blocks of stocks is too narrow for traders of the 100 to 500 share class.

3. There is no market, or at least only a nominal market for inactive stocks. Thus, it frequently happens that a stock will become the center of speculative activity on the Stock Exchange. If it is maintained, the Consolidated Exchange may take it up for a brief period, when with a cessation of activity on the Stock Exchange holdings of small amounts must make concessions on the Consolidated Exchange.

4. A few Consolidated Exchange houses charge 6 per cent interest throughout the year from the day of purchase. Among others the rate is usually higher than the Stock Exchange rate. During the period when the weekly settlement was in practice, there were no interest carrying charges for stocks from Monday until Saturday. Stocks carried over Saturday also carried one week's interest. The Exchange having unwisely adopted the daily clearing plan, interest is charged from the day of purchase. The plan of clearing stocks is identical with that of the Stock Exchange—balances in stocks are received and delivered each day.

There are fewer bucket shops on the Consolidated Exchange to-day than there have been in the past. Certain firms of this description find that they can secure more business through an Exchange connection than without one. Their business is transacted under the cloak of respectability. Such a house, for example, receives your order to buy 10 or 100 shares of stock. It employs on the Exchange five or ten brokers as necessity may require. The order to buy at a price is transmitted over the telephone to the Exchange and at the same time an order to sell at the same price is also transmitted. The two brokers then "come together" if they can and "match" or "bucket" the order. They know each other and endeavor to trade with each other, whenever possible. When this is not possible the buying and selling order is executed as near the first purchase or selling price as the market will permit. This is called "getting names." Having executed such a transaction, the firm in question finds itself in the position of a bucket shop—it has no liability on the Exchange. If the customer loses, the firm takes his margin; if the customer wins, the firm pays the loss. Another reason for this awkward method of conducting a bucket shop is that a customer of an Exchange firm can demand the names of the brokers to his transaction, and failing to get them, could complain to the Exchange. If the Exchange demanded them and they were not furnished, the firm would be liable to expulsion from membership. And again, the customer might insist upon the return of money lost on the plea that no transaction had been effected. The brokers executing such orders comply with the rules to all intents and purposes and the details of the complicated bookkeeping involved are worked out with great ingenuity. The business of this character on the Consolidated Exchange has reached proportions that have been responsible for much complaint. "Matched" or "bucketed" orders injure rather than help an exchange. Others, trading legitimately, are placed at a disadvantage and the value of such trade is best represented by a cipher. The speculator trading through such a firm takes serious chances on its financial responsibility, although a half dozen of them have weathered many financial storms. In closing out trades through such concerns, the customer frequently has to accept prices that are wide of the market, and when this is so, the broker has no hesitation in placing the fault—not with himself—but with the facilities of the Exchange which enables him to carry on his trade.

Young men—and older ones—who wish to speculate with the least possible expense buy Consolidated Exchange memberships, and trade for their own account. They have retired as clerks from Stock Exchange houses, are sons of Stock Exchange members or may be men of limited capital. They pay nothing in commissions. If they are "bears" on a "bear" market, they make money on their commitments by "carrying" stocks for the interest charges which they receive. If they care to lend money on stocks as collateral, they can average 6 per cent or better through the year, owing to the demand from brokers with small capital to have their stocks "taken up" and "carried" by some one else.

The trader is a speculator of the same type as the one described above. He, however, closes up his accounts each day. He returns to his home, neither "long" nor "short," and says that he sleeps better than if he were deep in the market. He trades for small profits—and small losses. His usual loss is ⅛ and he rarely assumes more than a ¼ loss. He has made a study of the demands arising from each group of brokers on his Exchange and he can usually "guess" the "next quotation" instinctively. He lives on the money lost through the legitimate commission houses, or his fellow traders and is a "gambler." He has no market opinions and simply follows the two Stock Exchange tickers, guided by the volume of Stock Exchange transactions and his knowledge of the same. He detests the bucket shop firms for the reason that when they match their orders it means that less money will be lost on the Exchange by the outside public than if the orders were actually transacted instead of "matched." He has the same feeling toward the trader who relies upon quick quotations.

The trader who relies upon quick quotations gets them in one of two ways. He has private and secret telephone connection with a fast Stock Exchange ticker or with a member of the Stock Exchange. There are few of these "wires." Such a broker will stand in a crowd and receive "finger" signals from the telephone boy of the rise and fall of prices and will buy or sell on the changes, slightly in advance of the blackboard and ticker quotations. At times traders of this type—who are very unpopular with other traders on the ground that they are taking an unfair advantage—have conducted profitable operations. They operate spasmodically, for a "wire" may be suddenly discontinued and as unexpectedly open up. Other traders who have not the advantage of these special facilities try to trail behind them. The work itself is hard on the nerves and few men stand it very long.

There are Consolidated Exchange houses which affect to transact an arbitrage business between New York, Philadelphia and Boston. They do not, however, appear to make very earnest bids for business in either city. The arbitrage business between the Consolidated Exchange, Boston and Philadelphia is not large at best. There are members of the Consolidated Exchange who say that they would like no better proposition than to be able to pay for a Stock Exchange membership, put a representative in that institution and arbitrage through the possession of superior quotation transmission facilities between the Consolidated and Stock Exchanges. An arbitrage house, such as the one described, must own at least several Exchange memberships and command comparatively large capital. The risk is great, for, if a member of the Stock Exchange were found guilty of conducting such a trade he would be promptly expelled from that institution. It is nevertheless true that there are brokers who risk their reputations in this way.

CHAPTER XXVI.

THE TIPSTER.

The novice in stock speculation, among his first inquiries, before making ventures, asks: "Is there any information that I can buy which will help me to make profitable deals?" The reply is in the negative, without qualification. There are two types of tipsters before the public.

1. The advertising tipster, man or woman, who advertises under fictitious names or assumes pretentious "information bureau" titles, and offers for sale advance information regarding stock market movements, and,
2. The tipster news bureau appealing to private subscribers and distinguished from the first group only by the fact that it does not advertise.

The tipster is a comparatively new figure in Wall Street. Ten years ago he would have been an impossibility. The amazing increase in wealth, the love of speculation peculiar to every people and a foolishly credulous public combined to open a field for the adventurer. His development has been rapid. Reputable newspapers have freely sold him their advertising columns. The United States Government not only fails to prohibit the use of the mails to him but in New York he has no difficulty in renting post-office boxes, and transacting business from a post-office box under an assumed name. Naturally many of these rogues had no wish to see their patrons, and so they were safeguarded by their post-office box connections, which rendered it unnecessary to advertise street and number addresses. This in itself should have been sufficient to warn sensible persons that the tipsters were disreputable thieves, but, strange to say, individuals and so-called "bureaus" at times obtained as many as 1,500 subscribers who paid $5 and $10 a month each for illiterate market letters.

A Brooklyn youth of the name of Miller, employed as a tool by a group of gamblers, organized on paper, what he called the "Franklin Syndicate." With the aid of shabby stationery and advertising from a 2-story frame house in a remote and poor section of Brooklyn, this young man succeeded in collecting more than $800,000 on his simple promise that he had discovered a successful method of speculating in the stock market and one which would enable him to pay his clients 520 per cent per annum. He was exposed as a fraud by the daily newspapers, and sentenced to a term of imprisonment in the State penitentiary, while those behind him succeeded in escaping to Europe with the bulk of the money. Men, women and children were among Miller's clients, while, curiously enough, the number of physicians was large. The desire to gamble at this time (1900) was intense. Many persons confessed that they knew Miller to be a fraud and that he could not honestly keep his promise, but they had hoped to be among the early investors who would have received all their original capital back and a profit too, in weekly installments, before the crash arrived.

Another man who had a commonplace Irish name and was in every respect a most commonplace person, advertised under a high-sounding English name for subscribers to his tips. To each subscriber he sent a wonderful telegraphic code, which he used as a medium in telegraphing his tips. His methods were so original; his advertising so specious, and the gambling fever so prevalent, that on the eve of the second election of McKinley he had 1,500 to 1,600 subscribers to his so-called "service." He notified his subscribers prior to Mr. McKinley's re-election that stocks were a "short sale," as, in his opinion, Bryan would be the victor as the result of a landslide. His subscribers were compelled on the election of the Republican candidate to buy back their commitments at figures which represented losses, and the wail of condemnation was so great that the Irish tipster retired from the field with from $75,000 to $80,000 and later engaged in the then profitable business of selling worthless oil stocks.

Still another representative of this type was the man who having 100 subscribers advised 50 to sell a certain stock short and the remaining 50 to buy the same stock. If 50 lost, his argument was that 50 had to win—an erroneous deduction—but he did not experience long life in the trade.

Another type included "confidential stenographers," "private wire telegraph operators," and "bookkeepers," who advertised inside information for cash in advance. Some of the tipsters were so crude and fraudulent in their methods that their advertisements became the laughing stock of Wall Street and yet many persons were and are to-day deceived by them. All "information" disseminated by group one is valueless. It is nothing more nor less than haphazard "guessing" by men absolutely lacking in self-respect.

Upon one occasion a Western adventurer, on coming to New York, was exposed in the newspaper with which the writer was identified as a member of its financial staff. He called with a letter of introduction from a broker and a very earnest request that he be allowed to live in peace as he had reformed and had engaged in no illegitimate business since his arrival in Wall Street. He had been one of the most audacious of the Western men who coined money from "tip" and "discretionary brokerage" operations. He was a fine looking, amiable fellow, and his statements were so ingenuous, and his letter of introduction so strong that there was no hesitancy in informing him that he would get no further publicity if he lived up to his promises. Profuse in his thanks he was about to depart when the writer remarked that if he fancied there was any obligation, it could easily be repaid by imparting some information about his old business.

"There is very little to tell," explained the tipster. "It is such a simple proposition. You see it is like this: Assume that I offer the public a sound, safe and absolutely reliable 6 per cent investment in the form of stocks or bonds for sale. I could advertise it through the newspapers or through the mails until I grew gray-headed before I could get rid of it to small investors—the class with which we do business, and always, preferably the man in the small town or the country. But, let me offer the public 40, 50 or 100 per cent, give me a good start and the use of the mails, and I assure you that I would have to hire a wagon in which to cart down Broadway my money-laden mail. Appeal to the cupidity of the small investor and you can get his money and in no other way. And I don't mind telling you that one reason why I have reformed is that I can no longer use the mails, having been shut out by order of the authorities."

In less than nine months a private detective who operates a bureau that is supposed to expose frauds called on the writer and made the statement that he represented the reformed tipster and had a proposition from him. He said: "Mr.------has been engaged in a legitimate brokerage business, not under his own name, but with another man. It is a discretionary business, 'mail order,' and no one has been robbed. Reporters have told him that he is going to be written up in to-morrow's paper. I will pay you $1,000 now if you will agree to stop the story."

The detective was requested to depart and invited not to call again, in which event he was promised that he too would be "written up." The editor of the newspaper interested was informed of the proposition, and the exposure was published the following day. The reformed tipster defaulted with profits estimated to exceed $100,000 and two "firms" closed up—(1) the "discretionary pool" brokerage house he directed and (2) the exchange brokerage house through which the tipster alleged he transacted his orders. The money was secured from out-of-town speculators on promises of dividends at the rate of 40 per cent annually and which, in the early stages of the game, are always paid regularly.

The tipster in group one is a "guesser" who has not even the advantages possessed by a first-class brokerage house. He is as far removed from the avenues that lead to desirable information as he is from those which lead to Paradise.

It is, indeed, a great pity that New York City has not produced a district attorney of force sufficient to break up this trade and bring the offenders within reach of the criminal law.

Type two is a somewhat different proposition. Tipster bureaus (called news bureaus) must be differentiated from the two excellent news bureaus[1] which supply Wall Street with news. The most charitable thing that can be said about them is that they do the best they can; that is to say, if their owners, by diligent work, gain early knowledge of manipulation in stocks they do not fail to make it known to their subscribers. They are also employed at times by manipulators, through the distribution of "Puts" and "Calls" to "boom" certain stocks and freely delude their subscribers to the best of their limited ability. It can be concluded without fear of contradiction that such information—as is all stock market information—must be very dangerous to the buyer.

A successful broker, watching a customer reading the market letters of one of the tipsters, remarked: "Why do you read that

---

[1]   Dow, Jones *&* Co., and the New York News Bureau.

stuff? Don't you know that to follow that fellow regularly a trader would go broke if he had the wealth of the Bank of England behind him?"

A Hebrew tipster, who has a considerable following, upon one occasion explained his business and his following in this way: "I occupy the same relation to the stock market that the doctor does to the patient. I diagnose the case, or in other words, with 20 years' experience and some knowledge of speculation, I investigate market conditions and draw conclusions. I try to obtain information whenever I can get it. I examine the fluctuations and volume of trading with care and govern myself accordingly. I am at my office early and late studying the market. It is true that I am almost always a bull. All my subscribers are bulls. I could not exist without them. I never predict declines unless we are on the verge of a panic or a bad break. If I think that a certain stock will decline I advise my clients to take profits. Such advice sounds well. I rarely advise 'short' sales, for experience teaches me that my clients will not make them. I am always positive—more positive when I am in doubt than when I am reasonably certain. No man can succeed in my business unless he is positive. Men who play this game want to follow a leader. They wish to be told to do things. They know that they cannot rely upon their own judgment. In a 'bull' market I can do better for them than many of them can do themselves. Am I often wrong? Yes. But I overlook my errors of judgment, as do my clients in constantly directing their attention and gaze to my successful tips. If a man wants to speculate let him do so. If he wants to buy and has a fancy, advise him as he wishes to be advised. If he buys and loses he will forget and forgive; but, if you advise him not to make the venture on which he had concentrated his mind, and the market movement favors his conception, then he will never forgive you for, in a majority of eases, he will hold you responsible for the loss of so much money. The stock speculative public is constantly changing. Novices to-day and veterans to-morrow. 'Flush' this year and 'broke' the next. The best we can do is to entertain them while they are here and try to give them a run for their money."

The cheerful humbug responsible for the above views disposes of his typewritten opinions for in round figures about $22,000 a year. That buyers are to be found for the product of the tipsters does not speak well for the intelligence of the buyers. Wall Street regards them with impatience and contempt and would suppress them if it could.

CHAPTER XXVII.

Conclusions of a Speculator.

A close student[1] of speculation in all its forms as conducted on the exchanges of this country has arrived at the following conclusions, which, he says, in application to speculation, are "universal laws." He divides his conclusions into two groups, laws absolute and laws conditional.

Laws absolute. *Never overtrade.* To take an interest larger than the capital justifies is to invite disaster. With such an interest, a fluctuation in the market unnerves the operator, and his judgment becomes worthless.

1. Never 'double up"; that is, never completely and at once reverse a position. Being "long," for instance, do not "sell out" and go as much "short." This may occasionally succeed, but is very hazardous, for should the market begin again to advance, the mind reverts to its original opinion and the speculator "covers up" and "goes long" again. Should this last change be wrong, complete demoralization ensues. The change in the original position should have been made moderately, cautiously, thus keeping the judgment clear and preserving the balance of mind.

2. "Run quick" or not at all; that is to say, act promptly at the first approach of danger, but failing to do this

---

[1] Financial Record.

until others see the danger hold on or close out part
of the "interest."

3. *Another rule is,* when doubtful *reduce the amount of
the interest;* for either the mind is not satisfied with
the position taken, or the interest is too large for
safety. One man told another that he could not sleep
on account of his position in the market; his friend
judiciously and laconically replied: "Sell down to a
sleeping point."

Rules conditional. These rules are subject to modification,
according to the circumstances, individuality and temperament
of the speculator.

1. *It is better to "average up"* [2] *than to "average down."* This
opinion is contrary to the one commonly held and
acted upon; it being the practice to buy and on a
decline buy more. This reduces the average. Probably
four times out of five this method will result in
striking a reaction in the market that will prevent
loss, but the fifth time, meeting with a permanently
declining market, the operator loses his head and
closes out, making a heavy loss—a loss so great
as to bring complete demoralization, often ruin.
But "buying up" is the reverse of the method just explained; that is to say, buying at first moderately and
as the market advances adding slowly and cautiously
to the "line." This is a way of speculating that requires
great care and watchfulness, for the market will often
(probably four times out of five) react to the point

---

[2] Pyramiding.

of "average." *Here lies the danger. Failure to close out at the point of average destroys the safety of the whole operation.* Occasionally (probably four times out of five) a permanently advancing market is met with and a big profit secured. In such an operation the original risk is small, the danger at no time great, and when successful the profit is large. This method should only be employed when an important advance or decline is expected, and with a moderate capital can be undertaken with comparative safety.

2. To *"buy down"* requires a long purse and a strong nerve, and ruin often overtakes those who have both nerve and money. The stronger the nerve the more probability of staying too long. There is, however, a class of successful operators who "buy down" and hold on. They deal in relatively small amounts. Entering the market prudently with the determination of holding on for a long period, they are not disturbed by its fluctuations. They are men of good judgment, who buy in times of depression to hold for a general revival of business—an investing rather than a speculating class.

3. In all ordinary circumstances my advice would be to buy at once an amount that is within the proper limits of capital, etc., "selling out" at a loss or profit, according to judgment. *The rule is to stop losses and let profits run.* If small profits are taken, then small losses should be taken. Not to have the courage to accept a loss and to be too eager to take a profit, is fatal. It is the ruin of many.

4. Public opinion is not to be ignored. A strong speculative current is for the time being overwhelming,

and should be closely watched. The rule is, to act cautiously with public opinion, against it, boldly. To so go with the market even when the basis is a good one, is dangerous. It may at any time turn and rend you. Every speculator knows the danger of too much "company." It is equally necessary to exercise caution in going against the market. This caution should be continued to the point of wavering—of loss of confidence—when the market should he boldly encountered to the full extent of strength, nerve and capital. The market has a pulse, on which the hand of the operator should be placed as that of the physician on the wrist of the patient. This pulse-beat must be the guide when and how to act.

5. *Quiet, weak markets are good markets to sell.* They ordinarily develop into declining markets. *But when a market has gone through the stages of quiet and weak to active and declining, then on to semi-panic or panic, it should be bought freely.* When, vice versa, a quiet and firm market develops into activity and strength, then into excitement, it should be sold with great confidence.

6. In forming an opinion of the market the element of chance ought not to be omitted. There is a doctrine of chances—Napoleon, in his campaign, allowed a margin for chances—for the accidents that come in to destroy or modify the best calculation. Calculation must measure the incalculable. In the "reproof of chance lies the true proof of men." *It is better to act on general than special information* (it is not so *misleading), viz.: the state of the country, the condition of the crops, manufactures, etc. Statistics are valuable, but*

they must be kept subordinate to a comprehensive view of the whole situation. Those who confine themselves too closely to statistics are poor guides. "There is nothing," said Canning, "so fallacious as facts except figures." *"When in doubt do nothing." Don't enter the market on half conviction; wait till the convictions are full matured.*

7. I have written to little purpose unless I have left the impression that the fundamental principle that lies at the base of all speculation is this: *Act so as to keep the mind clear, its judgment trustworthy.* A reserve force should therefore be maintained and kept for supreme moments, when the full strength of the whole man should be put on the stroke delivered.

CHAPTER XXVIII.

SUCCESSFUL AND UNSUCCESSFUL SPECULATORS.

Speculators may be divided broadly into two classes—those who are successful and those who are unsuccessful. The successful speculator when compared with the total number of speculators is in the small minority. This is a statement that can be established by an examination of any broker's books of accounts. Even in a bull market, the only market in which the outside speculator will trade freely, speculators for the rise lose money.

Almost all speculators are amateurs. They approach the market with confidence, score an initial success and then cast prudence to the winds. Failure is the result. It takes time to make a successful speculator, except under extraordinary circumstances. While simple purchases and sales are in themselves extremely easy, knowledge of stock speculation can only be acquired by experience. A 55-year-old Stock Exchange broker who won and lost three fortunes and yet managed to retire on a competency, remarked on one occasion: "A man usually quits this business at the time when he should begin to make money." This broker won his early successes in the days of Vanderbilt and Gould. Later he was unsuccessful, and in the markets of 1896 to 1902 his winnings were not notably heavy. Just prior to his retirement he said: "The market has changed since I was a young man. It is a much larger proposition. As I grow older I find that I lack the nerve of my youth. The younger men have the nerve and vitality which I lack. I love to trade and can make money in any market as a trader, provided the fluctuations are wide enough, but my judgment of prolonged price movement can no longer be relied upon, although I know men who are as correct in their market conclusions to-day as I was 15 and 25 years ago. I suppose that I am too much inclined to measure events by my old yard stick; in other words, I am behind the times."

A successful Hebrew speculator, a young man of 35, said during a discussion of stock speculation: "I started out in the dry goods business and recall the time when a dry goods merchant who speculated in stocks was regarded as an unsafe man by his friends and creditors. He was the exception, and yet to-day the merchant who does not speculate is probably the exception. The introduction of industrial stocks doubtless has had much to do with the changed conditions. In my opinion the man who comes to Wall Street without experience in stock speculation and in possession of a large sum of money will become bankrupt or crazy or both. Wall Street is no place for a man with money. The only man entitled to consider himself the possessor of hard common sense and the right attitude toward this business is the one who is satisfied to risk a very little money in an experiment to ascertain if he has the right temperament for a speculator, and, reasoning powers that can be successfully applied to market movements."

It would appear therefore that the successful speculator should have the knowledge gained through experience, a condition which is suggestive of a period of experimentation and losses. Judging from the view of the retired broker a man may have too much experience, but this experience will be an advantage to him in gaining a livelihood as a trader. From the Hebrew's point-of-view the speculator must experience the up-and-downs of victory and defeat before he can consider himself to be other than a novice.

It must not be concluded, however, that all experienced Wall Street men are successful speculators. Quite the contrary is true.

Many of the most successful brokers never speculate, experience having taught them that they do not possess those mental faculties required in the successful speculator. Other Stock Exchange firms, in their articles of co-partnership, require that no partner shall be permitted to speculate. It is also true that the financial critics, who write so knowingly and cleverly of market movements, are not successful speculators, insomuch as they are rarely men of wealth. If their market judgment were as sound and accurate as they would lead one to believe from a perusal of their articles, there is no reason why they should not be millionaires in fact, and yet, strange to say, financial journalism has not yet produced a millionaire speculator.

It is hardly reasonable, therefore, for the amateur speculator to expect to make successful ventures until he has had some experience, and this experience presumably will cost money. It certainly seems wise for the novice to reduce his early speculations to the minimum limit. If he contemplates trading in 100 shares, the preliminary ventures should be reduced to 10 when his theories of market movements and judgment may have ten tests at the cost of one 100 share venture. Undoubtedly one of the great roads to failure in stock speculation is the one which leads a speculator to trade on small margins, with no reserve; to score early success, and to enlarge his operations until he is so extended that the first serious decline turns profit into loss.

It has been said often enough that Wall Street—meaning the stock market—is reasonable; that in "the end reason prevails." What is meant is that after a prolonged period of fluctuation the price of a stock approximates its real money earning value. This value, however, fluctuates also with bad and good times. Values ultimately determine prices. Values are often hard to ascertain. They are more attainable in the railroad than the industrial quarter. The more obscure they are, the more violent the fluctuations;

and the more violent the fluctuations, the greater the risk of the speculator, especially the one who trades on a margin.

It may be asked by the seeker for principles; can safe and definite rules be formulated through known methods of reasoning by the speculator? Unquestionably the man with a logical mind, who can analyze *all* the factors governing price movements, has an immense advantage over the most common type, known as the "guesser." The successful speculator, however, must not only reason logically regarding transpired events, but he must anticipate the results of those that are coming. A man's reasoning may be accurate and even then his speculations are at the mercy of the "unexpected development" which has been the Waterloo for more than one unfortunate taker of chances.

If "the basis of inductive reasoning is the natural inclination of the mind to believe that whatever is true of a considerable number of individuals, will be true of the whole class to which these individuals belong," then the simple inductive reasoner will not succeed as a speculator, and yet in this class must be included most speculators. Their conclusions are hasty and not subjected to the test of further reasoning.

And if the speculator is to rely upon deductive reasoning on the belief that "whatever can be affirmed of an entire class can be affirmed of every individual of that class,

"he will find that he has many associates who have been flat failures. Nor can the stock market be unerringly judged by "demonstrative" or "probable" reasoning. It is true that the speculator does at times form premises that lead to accurate conclusions. The premises are the "mathematical or other self-evident truths."

In the practical work of the stock market premises are formed on statements and beliefs that may be called "probable truths"; they are supposed to be true and are believed. The conclusions in all such syllogisms, like the premises, however, are only "probable" truths, and so the "probability" factor becomes very important. The successful speculator can only accurately rate Wall Street statements of "probable truths" when he has acquired knowledge of stock market manipulators, and the speculative public. Most stock market speculative ventures are based on "loose reasoning" or bold guess work, hence the speculator contends not only with his own tendency to fallacious reasoning but with the sophistry of the manipulators and manufactures of stock. There has been discussion of speculators who possess "intuitive judgment." The idea that the market will undergo a change becomes an impulse, and straightaway the impulse becomes a venture. In speculation their theory is that "he who hesitates is lost," but the trader who possesses intuitive stock market judgment of value can be counted upon the fingers of one hand.

"Reasoning rests upon the ultimate basis of immediate and intuitive judgments," and the average stock speculator must stand or fall on the accuracy of his own conclusions. His powers of reasoning should be nicely balanced and adjusted. He should be a shrewd judge of "men, money and things." Reasoning, born of his own experience, is of the most permanent value. It is direct evidence. As a matter of fact, however, he is a trader generally on "circumstantial evidence," for which he has formed rules and which are chiefly remarkable for missing links. Reasoning by analogy must also be employed by the speculator who will find in all probability that like his fellow, he prefers others to do his reasoning for him when it becomes difficult.

In the stock market, as elsewhere, men love to follow a leader. They will take desperate chances on the opinions of others; on the merest hearsay, the most absurd rumor. They are as easily frightened as a flock of sheep and credulous to the point of stupidity. Men who are contemptibly mean in the matter of expenditures on themselves and their families will lose thousands of dollars in betting on a tip, and others who in their ordinary walks of business are sane and reasonable lose all their powers of reason on coming in contact with the "chance" to make "something for nothing."

"If," said a wealthy business man and a losing speculator, "I would be satisfied with the profits and losses I make in my own business I could become rich in Wall Street; but no, I am too greedy. That is the trouble with almost all men who speculate."

"My speculations," said a successful speculator "would be more successful if I kept faith with myself. In the morning I come down town promising myself to carry out a certain plan of campaign. I depart from it on a snap judgment. The sound conclusion was the one I should have adopted every time."

There is a type of speculator who has been making imaginary ventures based on the daily quotations. He is invariably successful. This is the same man who always tells his friends what to do, and what he and they might have made had his "judgment" been followed. The writer has met this man as he was about to test his judgment in the market itself—and after. Needless to say he has made no distinction between the two propositions, in one of which he is "out" of the market and the other "in." He ascertains that it is quite one thing to have his money in his pocket and another to have it staked upon the rise and fall of a stock. With his money up, he is swayed by the passions of the gambler. He is deluded by the sophisms uttered by the manufacturers of "news." He is impatient, stout and weak-hearted in succession, a creature beset by worry in a new form, and torn by a conflict of emotions that were absolutely foreign to him when he traded on paper and made money. A good stock market advisor may be a very poor speculator, as is frequently the case. The man who contemplates embarking upon the sea of speculation should carefully consider the psychological side of speculation.

A man may place a wager on a horse or a card. The decision is almost instantaneous or at the most requires but a few minutes. The mental strain and worry incidental to the decision that you win or lose is not of long or serious duration. In stock speculation the duration of your venture may be weeks or months. This factor of uncertainty and suspense, inducing worry and impairment of reasoning powers, increases or decreases in keeping with the temperament and capital of the speculator. He may be a "good loser" or a "bad loser." He may be rich and can afford the loss when his judgment will not be impaired or he may be relatively poor or unduly extended when his judgment becomes utterly worthless. Here we have the crux of the speculative proposition—a man may embark on his ventures backed by accurate powers of reasoning; but on making his hazard the suspense is unexpectedly prolonged or his margin is tested to the extreme point of elasticity, or there is some other unlooked for adverse influence when he succumbs to loss of nerve.

"Loss of nerve" is an expression often used in Wall Street. A man may be accurately diagnosing the stock market fluctuations and yet "lose his nerve" on the day or the week prior to the successful fruition of his commitment. But, having lost his nerve, he retires defeated and perhaps a loser. "Loss of nerve" is frequent among professional, but more common among amateur speculators, and it may be accompanied by a still worse symptom—loss of power to act—leaving the victim irresolute, undecided and the prey to hundreds of whims and fancies. In his observations the writer has known old and successful speculators to lose their nerve and liquidate their stocks on the "twaddle" of a loud-voiced, irresponsible reporter who talked of possible disasters during a temporary period of distress.

And again, it has been observed that a room can be crowded with small, happy, talkative speculators during a rising market and be succeeded by the same room crowded with gloomy, discontented, silent speculators during a slight decline. Enter the same room, during the decline, a "bear," vigorously outspoken, and the equanimity of the room and the nerve of the speculators is lost to the point that the manager of the office has difficulty in keeping his customers from needlessly sacrificing stocks, while the interval may be one of natural reaction.

The manager of a large commission office, where many hundred thousand dollars are lost annually, says: "I hate to see men lose money; but if they did not lose it here they would go somewhere else. This is the only business that I understand. I have made and lost a fortune in it. Now, although I am a young man (42), I would willingly sell out my chances for an annuity of $5,000 a year. Do I speculate? No. I prefer a good appetite, and sound sleep to a poor appetite and broken sleep. My friends think I am pretty clever, and so I am, but I am no cleverer than the large majority of speculators, although there are times when my judgment is much better than theirs Disinterested advice, under the circumstances, is better than their own judgment. Yes, of course the majority are losers. Most of them are unable to acquire the most simple and essential principle of the game, i.e., taking a small loss. In this contest men are not their normal selves. I refer now to the margin speculator who is gambling and governed by passion and excitement. He is far removed from myself, for example. I am cold and impassive, even during a panic, for I am not risking money. I must see to it that the firm does not lose money and we must sacrifice the gamblers with a strong hand—not because we like to, but because we have to. The successful speculator in the time of stress, I take it, should have the same control of himself as I have and I know very few speculators who are outwardly and inwardly calm when they are steadily losing and perhaps threatened with serious losses or even bankruptcy. I have not that control over myself, and that is why I lost my money.

"Then again, the average speculator buys stocks when they are 'strong' and sells them when they are 'weak.' This is a common principle with them and shows fallacious reasoning. In stock fluctuations, prices advance and decline, or vice versa, as it is a bull or a bear market. Therefore when a stock is 'strongest,' to the superficial eye, it is really 'weakest,' for then it should be sold for a reaction, just as it is sold by the so-called insiders. When outside buying orders are most numerous, a decline usually follows, and in the case of a bear market the conditions are precisely reversed."

During normal markets, brokers have observed that the psychological factor is so strong that speculators are not disposed to trade as freely and confidently in wet and stormy weather as they are during the dry days when the sun is shining, and mankind cheerful and optimistic. The average stock speculator is an optimist, and usually an enthusiast. He is on the constructive side of the account; he speculates for the rise. He is easily influenced—it may be by the weather or it may be by idle gossip, and frequently his cause of failure is due to temperamental shortcomings of his own with which his broker only is acquainted and to which he is absolutely blind.

The average man prides himself on his judgment. He is an egotist, a vain creature and places an exaggerated value on his own acumen. In the study of several hundred speculators the writer has observed that the amateur speculator, when he makes a winning on his broker's suggestion or advice, calmly and unhesitatingly compliments himself on his own excellent judgment. Per contra if the venture is a losing one he has no hesitation in blaming his broker for the error of judgment. He is always reluctant to acknowledge that the loss may have been due to his own error; in fact he places so high a value on his own judgment that in seeking for excuses for the loss the idea of blaming his faulty methods or reasoning capacity is the last idea which occurs to him. There is no broker of experience who is not familiar with this type.

Conceit in this form is probably responsible for the inability of the average speculator to accept small losses. Now the average speculator will take a 1 to 3 per cent profit and a 5 or 10 per cent loss. A speculator who pays ¼ commission for the round turn and interest charges—say ⅛ more—or ⅜ net on every hundred shares must make 1 per cent at least on every four transactions to be even with the game. That is his handicap, and it is a severe one. But it is a well-known fact that the penalty is not considered in this light. If, therefore, it is calculated along with the traders' tendency to take small profits and large losses, it will at once be acknowledged that the amateur who backs his "raw" judgment has a precarious foothold in the quicksand which has overtaken him.

The speculator will purchase a stock on, say, a 10 per cent margin. If it advances 1½ points he will likely take his profit. If it declines 1½ points he will hang on in the hope that he made no error of judgment, although he is somewhat doubtful. Should the decline be continued he will become even more doubtful, but as the loss is a substantial one, he is determined not to take it but to "hang on," as he is a fighter. Should the decline become more extensive, he, to use his own expression, becomes "obstinate." He "knows" that he is "right" and is determined to see "the thing through." And finally he probably closes the trade when his broker advises him to sell out or deposit more margin.

A successful speculator must make 1 per cent on every four trades to be even with the game, and he must exactly reverse the novices' usual procedure of taking large losses and small profits. If he finds on testing his capabilities that he cannot do so, then he should abandon the speculative field to others, as there is no profit in it for him.

Upon more than one occasion the writer has known of two persons trading through a commission house in this way. One would buy a stock at a price and the other sell it short at the same price and yet both lose money. For example, A bought 100 shares of Sugar at 124⅞ and B sold short 100 shares of Sugar at 124⅞, and for the moment this was the high price. Sugar the following day declined to 123, at which point A, becoming nervous, sold and lost $212.50 plus one day's interest. B, elated over the keenness of his judgment and his beautiful foresight, made his trade with the idea of securing a 1 per cent profit, but success emboldened him and he changed his plan and determined to hold on. Two days later Sugar had not only recovered its loss but had advanced to 128½, where the short stock was bought in at a loss of $362.50. So much for the judgment of the amateur speculator.

Again, it is to be observed that a manipulated stock breaks sharply. The object of the break may be to force out margin traders—to dislodge their holdings when the advance will be resumed. The margin trader will grimly contemplate the decline and finally, when a serious loss confronts him, will sell out. He has too much "company," for other speculators in the same predicament are doing precisely the same thing—selling out at a loss, which is exactly what the manipulators playing with known conditions want. The manipulators having secured the desired stock and resumed the advance the speculator reasons with himself after this fashion: "There, I told you so. I knew I was right about that stock. Didn't I say to myself that it would sell up to -- ----? Wasn't I convinced by what I knew that I had the right idea? Just my infernal luck. If I had only held fast and sat through the decline I would have been all right." Delusions again. There were many others who bought and sold under the same conditions. The decline would have been continued until all or most of the stock in question had been liquidated. The purchases of the margin speculators caused the manipulated decline. Their forced liquidation was necessary before the rise could be resumed. His *sale* of the stock induced the rally, or was at least a prerequisite. His purchase at the "top" helped check the rise and furnished fuel for a decline profitable to the manipulators. And yet in his own reasoning he has not considered himself as a factor contributing to the decline and aiding the subsequent recovery. In other words his judgment is wholly at fault; his conclusions were in error when the commitment was made and again following its consummation. He deceives himself so cleverly that the sophism of the manipulator is hardly necessary to add attractiveness and fascination to the struggle for money.

To stand in the office of a commission firm all day and hear the market opinions expressed and the reasons for making commitments is to understand why so much money is lost. The man who "guesses," who has a "fancy for a particular stock," who wishes "to make a bit," who has "a tip," is in the majority. He has the speculative fever, and having contracted the disease he has not the time nor the mood to adopt the reasoning dictated by ordinary common sense.

"Buy," says a customer to his broker, "100 shares of Metropolitan at 150."

The stock is bought at a cash cost of $15,000. The customer's equity in the stock is $1,000. The stock is capable of wide fluctuations.

"What did you buy it on?" the customer is asked.

"My friend Smith told me that it is going up."

"Who is Smith?"

"Oh, a neighbor of mine. He heard it was a good thing from Jones, whose cousin is a director in the company."

Would this man, who is A type, have invested $15,000 (equity $1,000) in his own business (mercantile) without a most careful investigation of conditions, and consequences, profits and losses, present and prospective? Would Smith and Jones influence him in such a transaction? Certainly not. And yet thousands of stock market ventures are made annually without any more justification.

Therefore if about to speculate in stocks, it behooves you to ask yourself if you possess the temperament and accurate and swift reasoning powers necessary to cope with the ablest money getters in the world. If you do, you will find that hardly a day passes that Wall Street does not present great opportunities for your skill in money making.

CHAPTER XXIX.

AN INTERESTING INQUIRY.

A correspondent asks for an explanation in detail of the meaning of "a large short interest," "a squeeze of shorts," "loaning rates for stocks," etc.

This inquiry implies some lack of comprehension of the principles involved in short selling, and as it comes from a banker, it is possible that others may be interested in a statement of how it is practicable to operate for a fall. The present form of operating for a fall is a modern device. It was preceded by a system of "buyers and sellers options" by means of which a buyer or seller acquired a right to deal at specified prices at dates more or less distant from the date of the contract. This, however, was a rather awkward method of trading and has ceased to exist in this market, except when it is unusually difficult to borrow stock.

In operating for a rise, only two parties are necessary for the contract. One buys and one sells. Delivery of the stock is made by the seller to the buyer; payment is received and the transaction is closed.

An operation for a fall, as carried on in the New York Stock Exchange, require three parties for its completion. Let us suppose that People's Gas is selling at par. A, although not the owner of any People's Gas, believes that the price will go lower. He, accordingly, offers a hundred shares of the stock at par. B accepts this offer and acquires the stock. A thereupon goes to C, who owns People's Gas, and borrows 100 shares, which A then delivers to B. B pays A $10,000, the price of 100 shares, and the transaction, as far as A and B are concerned, is at an end. But A, in order to obtain the use of the stock owned by C, has to deliver to C $10,000 as security for the return of the borrowed stock. Time elapses when it may be supposed that People's Gas has fallen to 95. A then buys of D 100 shares at 95, and, receiving the stock from D, returns it to C, the previous lender, and receives back from C the $10,000 deposited as security for the loan of the stock. A has, therefore, made $500 as the result of the operation for a fall begun with B.

A number of questions may be anticipated. Can A with certainty borrow stock from C? If C has the stock, and some one always has it, he is willing to lend it because there is little risk in so doing and because C gets the use of A's money, deposited as security, at lower rates of interest than C would have to pay for the use of the same amount of money if borrowed from a bank. Furthermore, if C borrowed $10,000 from his bank, he would be obliged to give as collateral securities valued at perhaps $12,000, whereas by loaning his stock to A he, in effect, procures a loan of $10,000 from A by the use of only $10,000 collateral.

The practice of borrowing and lending stocks is so universal that it is as much a part of the business to borrow stocks as it is to borrow money at the banks. The customer of an office has no trouble or difficulty on this account. He merely gives the order to sell, margins his account, and the broker arranges the terms of borrowing with his fellow brokers.

If there is a general impression that a stock is going to fall many people may sell it short at the same time. In this case, the borrowing demand may exceed the current supply. When this occurs the loaning rates fall. That is to say, A gives C the $10,000 as before described; but, on account of the demand for the stock, C does not pay as much interest. Assuming the money rate to be 4 per cent, the rate on borrowed stock under normal conditions might be 3½ per cent, but if the demand to borrow were quite large, the lender of the stock would have to pay only 2 per cent or even less for the money received as security.

If the demand to borrow were still greater, the stock would loan at what is called "flat," which means that no interest would be paid on the money deposited; or, with a still greater demand, A would be compelled not only to give C the use of the $10,000 without interest, but would have to give C an arbitrary sum, called premium, in addition for the use of the borrowed stock. Premiums range all the way from 1-256 up to 1 per cent or more a day—the latter, of course, only in very extraordinary cases. A premium of 1-16 of 1 per cent per day is as high as premiums often go even in a bear market. This means that A not only gives his money without interest, but pays C $6.25 per day for the use of 100 shares of stock. This premium is, of course, charged by the broker to the customer who is short of the stock.

Generally speaking, it is cheaper to operate on the short than upon the long side of the market. The interest account always runs against the operator for a rise, while the operator for a fall, selling a non-dividend stock, has no interest to pay, unless the short interest creates a premium. Some houses allow customers a part of the interest received on account of short sales. Traders usually operate more heavily upon the short than upon the long side, as it does not take as much capital, the money required in borrowing stocks being furnished by the buyer.

All this suggests the meaning of the term "squeeze of shorts." If a large number of people are borrowing stocks, those who lend the stocks know who the borrowers are, and in a general way, something of the amount which is being borrowed. The rules provide that the borrower can any day return the stock borrowed and receive back his money. The lender can any day return the money deposited and get back the stock loaned, in which case some other lender must be found.

When a bear campaign is under way, the owners of stocks see their property depreciate in value. They then sometimes form combinations for the purpose of calling in a large part of the stock loaned in some one day. The consequence is that the borrowers, being notified to return stock, look about for other lenders, and, finding the supply insufficient, are obliged to buy stock in order to get it for delivery, and this buying, coming suddenly, is apt to make a rapid advance in prices, especially as the bulls who have called in the stock usually join in advancing quotations.

This would seem to be a very dangerous position for the bear, but in practice squeezes do not usually last very long or cause very great fluctuations. There have been cases where a squeeze of shorts has sent the price of a stock up 30 or 40 points in one day. There have been a considerable number of squeezes which have advanced prices as much as 10 points in a day. Ordinarily, however, the total advance in a squeeze is not more than 4 or 5 points because the owners of stock, who understand the reasons for decline as well as anybody, take advantage of the rise to sell and the bulls, therefore, supply their bear friends with stock enough to make the required deliveries. The possibilities of this kind always make the short interest watched with more or less attention as containing the germs of advance not founded on value, but on the necessity of having stock to deliver.

A corner is a disastrous affair, very seldom occurring. It means that the bears in over confidence have sold more of a certain stock than there is in existence. It is, therefore, impossible for some of the bears to obtain stock for delivery and the bulls therefore are able to bid the price up to any figure which they like. It is theoretically possible for a bear to be absolutely ruined in a close corner, but such a thing is almost impossible in these days of large capitalization. The last close corner in the market was in Northern Pacific. A corner usually inflicts great loss upon the people who make one as well as upon the bears who are caught, and knowledge of this fact has led the great market leaders time and again to refuse to permit corners when the oversold condition of the market would have justified it. Mr. Gould could undoubtedly have made a close corner in Missouri Pacific in 1884, but he absolutely refused to permit anything more than a well sustained squeeze of shorts.

Broadly speaking, there is no more danger in being short of the market than in being long, although care should be taken to sell only stocks of large capital, which are known to have been distributed and in which trading is active. There is a little more difficulty in selling fractional lots short on account of the fact that it is sometimes necessary for the broker to borrow 100 shares in order to deliver 20 or 30 shares. Ordinarily, however, this is arranged with the odd lot dealers without difficulty.

The public as a whole avoids the short side, partly through not understanding it and partly through what seems to be a natural feeling against operating for a fall. Even among professional traders, there are many who have an instinctive feeling against the short side of the market. This, however, should be overcome by anyone dealing in stocks, inasmuch as the bear period is usually longer than the bull period and, in recent years an operator should have been a bear through at least half of every decade.

It has been said occasionally that bears never make fortunes. There are exceptions to this rule, and, so far as it is a rule, it is due to the fact that the general development of the country has had a tendency to bring out whole people who stayed long of securities even through a reorganization. This will probably be true to a certain extent in the future. Nevertheless a great deal more money has been lost on the long side of stocks than was ever lost on the short side. There is no sound reason against operating for a fall, when a bear period is under way.

CHAPTER XXX.

STOCK MARKET MANIPULATION.

The machinery of a "pool" in stocks and the process of "working" the market is described as follows by an experienced manipulator.

"It is only fair to say that the public rarely sees value until it is most markedly demonstrated to them, and the demonstration comes generally at a pretty high price. It is easier for them, as experience shows, to believe a stock is cheap when it is relatively dear, than to believe it is cheap when it is more than cheap. A Stock Exchange operator or group of operators decides, we will say, that a certain stock is selling cheap—that is, below value. Value means, in Stock Exchange speculation, intrinsic value, plus future value, plus the additional Stock Exchange value. A large holder of the stock begins by going around to other large holders. Ownership is counted, and the outstanding stock in public hands fairly estimated.

"The first necessary detail is to 'tie up' in a pool these known holdings, in order to prevent realizing sales by larger interests. If such large holdings cannot be kept off the market, hands are joined in certain direction, and a long and patiently worked-out plan of accumulating the stock at low prices, before tying it up, is devised. This takes the form of manipulation within a certain range of prices. It may be assisted by natural stock-market conditions, which encourage sales by outsiders at a sacrifice. Frequently persistent attacks on the stock by the people who wish to buy it are undertaken, which bring out miscellaneous public holdings, and which, if carried sufficiently far, dislodge even

146

important inside holdings. To accomplish the decline, matched orders are frequently used, whereby the pool really sells to itself. Large offerings of the stock are also continually placed on the floor with no takers, resulting in the gradual lowering of commission-house selling limits, and the securing of cheap stock thereby.

"The question of borrowing money is important. A pool can rarely do the whole thing with its own capital. It is assumed that the money-market outlook favors a stable condition, for it is idle to suppose such operations would be conceived were conditions pointing otherwise. Money brokers have, of course, been employed by the house handling the pool, to borrow from the banks large amounts of time and short-time call money, termed 'special loans,' on which the collateral is largely to be the security in question, and on which loans a liberal rate is paid and liberal margins given.

"The 'publicity department' must also have been covered. Practically all important pool operators keep on hand this appendage to their work. The 'gossip' affecting the stock must be printed, and this department is systematized to a degree few suspect. It is generally in charge of a man intimately connected with newspaper channels, covering every important city, if need be, and this person receives a large compensation for the duty performed of distributing for circulation, when the managers of the pool see fit, items of news and gossip affecting the stock. The 'insiders' being in the pool, every item of news is carefully bottled up, and distributed only at what is thought to be the right time. The need for this will be apparent when it is observed that explanation must be made for advances and excuse for declines in all manipulated stocks. The fact that insiders and the pool own the news, so to speak, and can thus discount its effect ahead of those who get it through 'publicity' channels, involves a moral point of view which has often been the subject of Wall Street discussion.

"The machinery of Stock Exchange work varies little. Orders are given to different sets of brokers from time to time to buy the stock, sometimes carefully and quietly, sometimes by openly and aggressively bidding for it, and vice-versa on the selling side. Rarely is one broker alone allowed to remain conspicuous on either side for any considerable length of time. All these transactions are 'cleared' by the brokers filling the orders; that is, instead of 'giving up' the names of their principals in the trades, they take in and deliver the stocks themselves, and then receive and deliver them from and to their principals.

"Market conditions now being favorable to the 'deal,' and emission of favorable news facts having resulted in public interest, the commission-house broker, who represents the 'public,' begins to be in receipt of many requests for opinion on the stock made active. The commission-house broker is a pretty good judge of the situation generally, and has spent his life studying values and watching manipulation. He thus assists in the operations by advising purchase. As a general rule, the advice falls flat, and few orders come out of it. But the pool continues; they are at present really buying stock and selling little. Some of these are actual trades, some are matched orders, but it is impossible, even for the brokers in the crowd, to tell which of such orders they may be. The result, however, is a marked stimulation of public interest, and commission-house buying orders begin. More news is published, and the deal becomes public talk.

"When this condition is created, the stock is up several points, and the pool begins to figure on selling. The machinery of the publicity department is then worked to its utmost extent, and the following morning finds a general demand for the stock from all commission houses. This is the time when a 'widespread' opening is figured on. Orders by the thousands are put in on the selling side, distributed to many brokers, with, of course, some buying orders also put in to a limited degree to 'take it as offered' at the opening. The 'high opening' is effected, and stock sold by balance sufficient to warrant pool support and renewed buying, after the overnight public orders have been filled. Then follows bold, aggressive buying by the pool in large quantities, aided by matched selling orders, and the volume of the business done attracts attention everywhere, and leads to enormous absorption by the public.

"Given favorable conditions, the public buying thenceforward controls the market, and the pool places only 'supporting' orders in the stock from time to time, when outside interest flags. This public buying will continue until it has carried the price so much beyond value that the pool can afford to liquidate freely. From then on, the operation proceeds to its profitable close, the various official, semi-official, and 'inside' announcements of news and suggestions covering the outlook in the immediate and near future—affecting the value of the stock, dividends to be paid, bond conversions, new alliances, consolidations—are the only necessary machinery."

Discussing "manipulation," Mr. Charles H. Dow says:

"In a broad sense, trading on the Stock Exchange represents the operation of supply and demand as applied to securities. Ordinarily, however, a comparatively small part of the business is done by investors. The larger part is the outcome of professional trading and of the manipulation that is carried on by large interests to accomplish desired results.

"Trading in stocks can ordinarily be divided into professional and public dealings. There is a great difference between the two. Professional trading includes manipulation and the operations of those who make trading in stocks a considerable part of their daily business. Trading by the public covers investment business and a form of dealing which is partly speculative and partly investment. The professional operator trades all the time. Public trading is variable and very uncertain.

"The two extremes in the market are occupied by manipulators who either wish to buy or to sell in considerable quantity, and the public which, in the end, wishes to invest wisely. The manipulator, therefore, looks to the public to buy the stocks which he wishes to sell, or to sell those which he wishes to buy. A large proportion of all manipulation is aimed at the public, and professional traders are merely the middlemen who try to take profits out of the movements which manipulators appear to be trying to make.

"Suppose that a syndicate finds itself with a profit in the form of $10,000,000 worth of stock. The way to convey this profit into cash is to sell the stock. The syndicate, therefore, makes an arrangement with some skilled manipulator, who undertakes to induce the public to buy this stock. He begins by seeing that the merits of the case are stated as fully and as widely as possible.

"Whether the stock is intrinsically valuable and the enterprise sound or unsound makes a great difference as to the class of men which undertake the manipulation, but it makes but little difference as to the methods which are employed to secure public buying. In any event, the first thing is to have the property known about and talked about. The way to obtain this result is to have the stock do something which makes brokers and speculators and writers try to find out what is causing the movements which are recorded on the tape.

"Manipulators in such cases usually tell friends that the stock in question is to be made active and advanced. This brings buying of a professional class, because it is understood that a deal of the magnitude proposed cannot be accomplished without sustaining the market for the stock for a considerable time during which trading in it will be comparatively safe. Manipulators know, furthermore, that one of the best ways of getting a stock talked about is to have people tell friends that they have made money by buying it. Accordingly, there is almost always money to be made with a minimum of risk in the early stages of such a campaign.

"The manipulator must keep the stock active, buying and selling from ten to twenty thousand shares a day in order to keep traders confident of a market on which they can sell, if at any time they become alarmed. It is characteristic of the public to buy on advancing prices rather than on declining prices. A stock which is to be sold is therefore kept strong and advanced moderately if the general market will permit this to be done.

"The larger the manipulation, the larger will be the volume of professional trading, and the greater the likelihood of the public taking an interest in the stock. Usually in such cases the public buying is at first small; then it becomes more confident, and finally there is full confidence and the stock is rapidly unloaded upon the public buying. Then the activity dies out, professional trading becomes less, and the public is satisfied or dissatisfied with its bargain, as the case may turn out.

"This occurs to a greater or less extent in the market all the time. There is always some large interest which would like to have the public buy or sell, and manipulation is going on with that end in view. Large interests know that if the public can be induced to trade freely in stocks which are of unquestioned value, they can generally be led into other stocks; therefore, an attempt is often made to get the public into the market by advancing three or four leading stocks. If the public comes in, the market is widened. If the public does not come in, the manipulators discontinue their efforts to make a market after a few days and wait for a more opportune time.

"The rule for the public ought to be essentially the rule which is followed by professional traders. When a stock is made active, consider it first with reference to its value. If it is intrinsically cheap, it can ordinarily be traded in as long as it is kept active. But it is generally wise to sell when activity ceases. If the stock is apparently above its value, a good deal more caution ought to be exercised about going in, and stop orders should be used to guard against severe drops.

"Generally speaking, manipulation in a new property is for the purpose of selling; in an established property, bull manipulation is usually discounting some favorable news which insiders are holding back. Bear manipulation in perhaps eighty per cent of cases is the discounting of something which is unfavorable. In twenty per cent perhaps, it is for the purpose of accumulating stock with reference to a succeeding rise.

"As a whole, however, bear manipulation is founded on knowledge that the stock under treatment is intrinsically dear. It is not, as a rule, good judgment to buy stocks which are under attack until the attack ceases and there are indications of a rally on the short interest which may have been made by those who followed the decline."

And again discussing a campaign in stocks, Mr. Dow says:

"The stock market alternates between periods of activity and periods of rest. Its periods of activity are usually started by manipulation and continued by a mixture of manipulation and public buying. Professional traders and the public usually try to follow the lead of some individual or clique which is apparently advancing some particular stock or stocks.

"The main difference between manipulators and general traders is that the manipulator endeavors to take advantage of conditions which he thinks will exist in the future. He believes that the condition of money or change in the value of a particular stock or something else will cause a given security to be worth more three months hence than it is now. He buys stocks quietly and then advances the price slowly or rapidly, as the case may be, with the expectation that the public will take his stock off his hands when it sees what he saw at the beginning. Whether the public does this or refuses to do it determines the success of the campaign.

"In a majority of cases, a well sustained advance supported by large trading will bring enough outside buying to enable a manipulator to unload a substantial line of stock. The speculative public always buys on advances and seldom on declines, in which respect it differs from the investing public which buys on declines and sells on advances. One of the most skillful manipulators in Wall Street says that any stock possessing merit and having some influential fact to be made the basis of a campaign can be marketed at an advance in price, if the manipulating interest is willing to pay the cost of such a campaign, which would perhaps average $250,000.

"This cost is chiefly applied to the creation of a market. The rules of the Stock Exchange do not permit A to tell B to buy stock from C at a given price, but it does not prohibit A from telling B to buy 10,000 shares of a given stock and at the same time telling C to sell 10,000 shares of the same stock. The results of such an operation would show that many brokers had participated in the trading, through a wish to take either the buying or the selling side, and that on the whole the market, although artificial in one sense, had been legitimate in the sense that anybody had a chance to step in and buy or sell at the price established.

"A bull campaign in the market is a far bigger under-taking than a campaign in one stock, because many stocks have to be moved. On the other hand, it is sometimes easier because it invites co-operation from many sources, and sometimes a very small amount of encouragement in a stock is sufficient to induce its friends to do all that is required to promote an active speculation.

"The general progress in a bull market is for the manipulating interest to take two or three prominent stocks, and by making them active and higher attract attention to the fact that a campaign has been started. It is customary to take stocks of the best class, in which there is a large investment interest and where the supply of floating stock liable to come on the market is known not to be large. This is why St. Paul is so often used as a leader, and why closely held stocks like Rock Island, Northwest and others of that class are frequently advanced materially at the beginning of a bull campaign.

"After stocks of this kind have been put up from 5 to 10 points, it is customary to shift the trading to stocks of the middle class on the idea that the public will not buy where there has been very large advances or where prices are very high, but will buy the cheaper stocks, even if they are intrinsically dearer. After stocks of this kind have been carried up a few points, it is customary to take up stocks of still lower price. It was considered for many years that when manipulators moved Erie, the end of a period of rising prices was at hand, because Erie was regarded as of next to no value and putting it up was considered diversion of the public, while other stocks were being sold.

"In a prolonged bull campaign, after the manipulators have moved the low priced stocks, they sometimes go back and move the others all over again, following the same order—the high priced stocks first, stocks of the middle class next, and then the cheapest on the list."

CHAPTER XXXI.

THE RECORD OF FIVE PANICS.

R ecorded below are the movements of a few active
stocks in the panics of 1873, 1884, 1893, 1895 and
1901. The figures include the high prices prevailing
shortly before the panic, in some cases those the day previous,
and in others several days prior thereto. The low prices are the
low points in the panic. The recovery given is to prices established
within a week or the low point in the panic, coming in some cases
within a few days and others not until nearly a week afterwards.

We are accustomed to think of the panic of 1873 as a very
serious event. It was sufficiently serious to compel the closing of
the Stock Exchange, but the decline outside of Lake Shore and
Western Union, seems singularly small in view of losses which
have been seen since. The panic itself was the culmination of
a feverish market which had lasted all the week, the final break
coming on Saturday. The average decline in that panic for nine
active stocks was 10.32 per cent. Figures follow:

1873 Panic.	High.	Low.	Decline.	Recov'y.
N. Y. Central.........	95	89	6	6
Erie	56⅛	50¾	5⅜	2⅜
Lake Shore	88	68	20	11
Wabash	50	42½	7½	7
Rock Island	95	86	9	10¼
St. Paul.................	37½	30	7½	5½
Lackawanna	92½	86	6½	7⅛

Western Union...... 76   54¼   21¾   19¼

The panic of 1884 reflected a larger average movement of prices, the losses of May 13-16 running from 8 to 15 points. The panic proper covered two days, while the recovery for ten stocks amounted to about five-eighths of the loss. Details follow:

1884 Panic.	High.	Low.	Decline.	Recov'y.
Lake Shore	94	81	13	8⅞
Rock Island	116¼	109½	6¾	6¼
St. Paul	77	65	12	7⅝
Burlington	118	114¼	3¾	3¾
Louisville	44	30¼	14¾	5
Missouri Pacific	80	65	15	7½
Union Pacific	50	41½	8½	3⅞
Western Union	60	51¾	8¼	5⅞

The panic of 1893 was not very severe in the extent of the losses. The average fall in 13 stocks was 7.34 per cent, and in only a few cases did the loss exceed ten points. In the leading stocks quoted the losses were from 7 to 9 points, while the recovery was in nearly every case larger than the panic decline.

1893 Panic.	High.	Low.	Decline.	Recov'y.
Burlington	74	69¼	4¾	10¾
St. Paul	52	46⅜	5⅝	9
Rock Island	58	53	5	8¼
Louisville	53	47½	7½	10⅛
Missouri Pacific	23	16½	6½	6½
Sugar	73	66¾	6¼	8⅜
Chicago Gas	53	43½	9½	8¾
Western Union	75	67½	7½	10⅝

The Venezuela panic of 1895 was about equal in intensity to the panics of 1873 and 1884. The average of 15 stocks fell 9.72 per cent, and a considerable proportion of the losses exceeded 10 points. The recovery was normal, about two-thirds the amount of the decline.

1895 Panic.	High.	Low.	Decline.	Recov'y.
Burlington............	197⅞	178	21⅞	14½,
St. Paul.................	72⅜	60½	11⅞	7½
Rock Island..........	72½	59	13½	10
N. Y. Central........	98	90½	7½	7¼
Louisville..............	49⅛	39	10⅛	6¼
Missouri Pacific.....	27⅝	19½	8⅛	6¼
Jersey Central........	105½	93	12½	8¼
Sugar	100½	92	8½	7⅞
Chicago Gas..........	68½	57½	11	7⅞
Western Union......	88¼	82½	5¾	4¼

The following shows the fluctuation in a few stocks in the panic of 1901:

1901 Panic.	High.	Low.	Decline.	Recov'y.
Atchison com........	90¼	43	47¼	33
Burlington	199⅝	178	21⅝	14½
St. Paul.................	188	134	54	29½
Rock Island..........	169⅞	125	44⅞	28
Louisville..............	111½	76	35½	27¾
Manhattan	131¾	83	48¾	32¾
Missouri Pacific.....	116¾	72	44¾	36½
N. Y. Central........	170	140	30	15

Union Pacific.........	133	76	57	47½
Amalgamated Copper	128½	90	38½	32
Tobacco	130⅞	99	31⅞	25¾
People's Gas...........	119½	98½	21	13¼
U. S. Steel com......	55	24	31	22

The declines are amazing when compared with the losses in other panics. Drops exceeded 40 points each in Atchison, St. Paul, Bock Island, Manhattan, Missouri Pacific and Union Pacific. The figures showing the high point were in some cases a week or more before the low point, but the drop as between the close, May 8th, and the low point, May 9th, covered in most cases a large proportion of the total decline.

The recovery was equally noteworthy. Union Pacific fell 57 points and rose 47½ points within one week. Missouri Pacific fell 44¾ points and recovered 36½ points in the same time. Other changes were almost as pronounced, going to show that in the extent of the fluctuations the panic this month was not to be named in the same breath with any panic record in the past.

It came and went so swiftly as to leave onlookers almost dazed. The speed and the extent of the recovery was all that saved the panic from being a financial catastrophe.

A long train of ills followed the smaller declines in panics past. The ills would have been a calamity had the low prices of May 9, 1901, continued for twenty-four hours.

The fluctuations of the May 9 panic show that while investment stock was not greatly disturbed and while commission houses proved to be strong enough to endure the strain without failure, the large trading which had been the feature of the market that year resulted in a rush to sell which carried prices far below what the decline would have been under normal selling pressure.

In other words, a great market represented by transactions of from two to three million shares a day, carries with it the possibility of movements in prices as much greater than normal as is the volume of trading greater than normal. There is a relation between the volume of business and the movement of prices. Great activity means great movements whenever the normal balance between buyers and sellers is violently disturbed.

CHAPTER XXXII.

End of Several "Booms."

The 1902 autumn collapse of numerous stocks, inflated in the progress of the crazy "boom" of that season to the highest prices on record, suggested reminiscences. There are many of such reminiscences in point.

The first half of 1881 was a period much resembling the first four months of 1901. Burlington and Quincy had risen 22½ points, St. Paul 28, Northwestern 23, Lake Shore, 17¾, Louisville 59½, New York Central 27½, Panama Railway 60, Western Union 57. This is the account of the period by a conservative reviewer of the time:

"In the present era, consolidation is the word, and nothing in the financial world has now such charms for investors and capitalists as this magic term. Let the stocks of two non-competing companies each be selling at 20, with few buyers; let a consolidation be proposed, share for share, and immediately the stocks are run up to 30—40—50—as the case may be. Add one more element to the transaction—water—in the shape of a stock distribution of 100 per cent or more, and the original amount of stock, selling for only 20, is found to be worth par. This illustration may present an extreme view of the case in the details mentioned, but the general fact is indisputable that a large number of stocks on roads that have never paid a dividend, nor have any prospect of paying one for some years to come, are now selling at 60 to 100, which last year were considered dear at 20 to 40."

There was a somewhat familiar ring to the description when applied to markets of 1901-2.

President Garfield was shot on July 2. A railroad rate-war broke out almost the next week; following which, the hot winds ruined the corn crop. All these occurrences were described, as usual, as "thunderclaps from a clear sky." The markets collapsed, with intervals of support from "inside interests." By autumn, stocks were down as a rule 10 to 20 points, the intervening decline having been much more severe.

In most respects, 1882 resembled 1902 exactly as 1881 resembled 1901. The "boom" of 1882 occurred later in the year. Up to midsummer, advances of more than 10 points or thereabouts were not numerous. September's high level, however, showed upward movements such as 33 in New Jersey Central, 24 in St. Paul, 34 in Lackawanna, 23 in Illinois Central, and 58 in Manitoba. From then until November, prices hung fire; they even scored "marked advances," with the help of rumors from Mr. Vanderbilt. On November 18 money was described as "easy and in a normal condition." On Monday, November 20, it rose to 20 per cent; it touched 30 later on. The surplus bank reserve had vanished, and a deficit of $3,000,000 took its place. It was said in a contemporary journal on November 25:

Stock market fluctuations have been so violent that feeling has almost verged on panic. The two points are the railroad war and the condition of the steel trade. Production of steel rails was enormously stimulated by rapid railroad building and the high tariff, and profits of manufacturers for a time were fabulous. It was a foregone conclusion (this was written long after the event) that mills could not keep up these profits.

They certainly did not keep them up, and depression was very severe, with a number of leading mills closed down during the autumn. The close of the year showed some such declines from the earlier autumn prices as 19 in Burlington and Quincy, 23 in Lackawanna, 11 in New York Central, 18 in Union Pacific,

22 in Manitoba, 23 in Pullman, 25 in Oregon Navigation. This was the last of the "big booms" of the period.

Passing over a long series of minor "booms," such as those of 1885, 1886, 1890, and 1895—nearly all of which were upset by the money market's rebellion against the excesses of the speculators—we come to 1899. The famous "Flower boom" was one of the most hollow in the entire series. It now appears laughable that the hopes of a great-market should have been pivoted on such a stock as Brooklyn Rapid Transit, but so it was. The genial atmosphere of the commission office where stock-jobbing "tips" were distributed to the unwary had its effect on the whole community and on the whole stock list. "Brooklyn" itself rose not quite 60 points; but there were other advances like the 25-point rise in Burlington, New Jersey Central's advance of 25, Lackawanna's 22, Manhattan Elevated's 36, Metropolitan's 81, and New York Central's 20. The chief manipulator died suddenly on May 13. None, or practically none, of the wind-bag stocks were found in his vaults by his executors. He at least had sold out what he had; but the public was left to sell the rest. The bell-wether stock of the entire list fell 37 points within a day, and has never touched its high price since. Manhattan Elevated dropped off 28 points of its recent inflated price, Metropolitan 54, and the standard railway shares some 15 to 20 points. The new-fledged industrials, which had shared in the happy movement, tumbled in similar proportion. The interesting fact of the "boom" of 1899 was that the money market played little part in tripping up the Stock Exchange.

CHAPTER XXXIII.

DEALING IN UNISSUED STOCKS.

Trading in unissued securities, in advance of their actual distribution, started in this country in connection with the issue of the new Government 4 per cent bonds, which were bought by the Morgan-Belmont syndicate on February 19, 1895. A somewhat similar practice had previously been in vogue in Europe, having originated in the desire of investors to arrange for the purchase of bonds or stocks in advance, when new issues were expected to come out. They naturally appealed to their banker to put through the transaction, and it came to be a common thing to fix upon the price which investors were to pay. This naturally led to trading in contracts for the new securities, based upon the estimated value which different persons thought they were worth.

Messrs. Morgan and Belmont had so arranged the terms for the flotation of the $62,315,000 of new Government 4s—so they thought—that those placed abroad would not be resold to this country right away, which would tend to defeat the purpose for which they were issued. But the foreign bankers were experts at disposing of securities before they were issued. Before the Secretary of the Treasury had put out the first lot a large number had changed hands at a sharp advance in price, and in many instances the original buyers never saw the securities which they had turned over. What they were really dealing in were contracts to deliver United States Government 4s, "when, as, and if issued." The syndicate got the bonds at 104½ and offered them to the public at 112¼ on the next day. On February 25, only 5 days after the offer to the public, trading in the new bonds, "when issued," began in the unlisted department of the Stock Exchange, the initial sale being at 118⅛, or 5⅞ above the price at which they were offered to the public. The price ran up to 1193/8 before the end of the week. On March 14, when the first bonds appeared, the price did not go above 120.

While there was much of a speculative character about the trading in the new bonds, most of the buying above 118, before the securities were issued, represented the execution of orders for investors who had failed to get any when they were offered at 112¼, and who thought they might have to pay still higher prices after the certificates came out. In this case they did not gain much by buying the "when issued" contracts.

The trading in Government bonds before issued opened up to American traders visions of great possibilities in getting an early start in new securities, and when the reorganizations of Northern Pacific, Reading, Atchison, and other railroad properties came along a little later dealing in contracts became a common thing on the Broad Street curb. For a long time the foreign bankers, who are experts in figuring out the niceties of "arbitrage" and of exchange transactions, did most of the business in the "when issued" contracts. One of their number says that profits of from $25,000 to $50,000 were sometimes made in a single security before the certificates came out. They made large amounts out of Northern Pacific, but some of them came out with a small loss on Atchison bonds and stocks, because they had made a mistake in not allowing enough margin for interest. Interest is a very important item. The method of operators consists in buying the old shares and selling the prospective new ones against the former. In determining the price at which to sell, the new the interval of time before the new are issued is taken into consideration, since interest must be paid on the shares which have been bought, and they must be carried until they can be exchanged. The trouble in the case of the Atchison was that the new securities did not come out until a later time than had been expected.

The important part which contracts for securities "when issued" may play, was perhaps best illustrated by the first transactions in those of the United States Steel Corporation on the Broad Street curb. These prices really determined the movements of Federal Steel, Steel and Wire, and other subsidiary shares on the Stock Exchange. For several days it was not known just what the old shares ought to be worth in the exchange for new, and they fluctuated wildly until the relationship was determined by watching the prices of United States Steel shares when issued. The common started on the curb at 38, and the preferred at 82¾ in the second week of March, last year. That an investor benefited by buying before issued seemed clear from the fact that when the new shares came out and they were introduced on the Stock Exchange, on March 28, the common started off at 42¾ and the preferred at 92¾. From the standpoint of the person who wanted to buy the old shares and sell the new against them it was a difficult task, because of the restrictions placed upon the exchange of securities. Some of the traders tried a little of what was termed "arbitraging" between the Stock Exchange and the curb, figuring out, as they thought, a profit of 4 or 5 points, but they gave it up when they realized how completely the syndicate controlled the situation.

The dangers sometimes incident to trading in unissued securities are illustrated by the San Francisco bond case (1902) and that of the United States Steel bonds, which it was proposed to issue, partly for the retirement of preferred stock and partly for betterments. Syndicate agreements provide, as a rule, that the participants shall take their proportion of the new securities issued, and find a way to dispose of them. It has been a common habit for syndicate members to make contracts for the sale of the securities 'when, as, and if issued," so as to get them off their hands as soon as possible. In the case of most of the companies promoted or reorganized by Mr. Morgan, the syndicate members were expected to take their proportion of the securities, unless it was specifically agreed that the managers were to dispose of them. No negotiable certificates were issued permitting of the transfer of subscriptions, as in the case of the San Francisco Street Railway Company, financed by Brown Brothers & Co. The subscriptions of the latter are dealt in on the curb; exactly like stocks.

The trouble in the case of the 'Frisco bonds doubtless arose from the fact that the agreement provided that the members should take the stock to which they were entitled. They might also be compelled to take the new bonds unless the bankers were able to sell them to better advantage—or such part as the bankers did not sell. It was possibly inadvertence on the part of the subscribers that caused them to sell the new 'Frisco bonds, not knowing whether they would have the certificates to deliver; or, they may have thought there would be "enough to go around" when $20,000,000 were issued. The small amount of San Francisco bonds that came out at the start, as well as the possibility that only $50,000,000, instead of $250,000,000 of United States Steel bonds might have been issued, illustrate two of the dangers that may arise from selling securities in advance. In the one case a temporary scarcity rendered it possible to run the price up to a fictitious figure, assuming that the contract was literally enforced which compelled the seller to deliver them the moment they were issued. In the second instance, a smaller issue of United States Steel bonds would render it necessary for the seller to deliver a really more valuable security than he thought he had sold, and he might have to take a loss.

Of course, there is always the risk that plans may be changed and the securities will not be issued at all. A notable instance which caused quite an uproar was the announcement of a new issue of India stocks by the British Government some years ago. These were extensively traded in "when issued," but the Government changed its mind, and all of the transactions had to be declared off.

CHAPTER XXXIV.

The Tipster's Point of View.

The stock market from the tipster's point of view is not uninteresting. As a guide, however, he is invariably less valuable than an honest broker, and is usually very clever in "calling" market movements after they have run their course.

The following "study" of stock speculation is the work of an advertising tipster, and the reader will be his own judge of its value.

WALL STREET'S GREAT GAME.

Over 90 per cent of the transactions on the Exchange are purely speculative—mere betting on quotations. So, likewise, 90 per cent of the fluctuations are based on manipulation, and not on the values of the properties or outside conditions. Good or bad crops have a very close relationship with the country's actual prosperity, and should be the paramount factor in stock market values; but the insiders are supreme in Wall Street, and manipulate prices up and down without much regard for crops, earnings or any outside factors. Nobody can shut his eyes to the fact that in a bull market (that is, when insiders are long), stocks go up in the face of bad news, and in a bear market (insiders short), prices go down, no matter how rosy the outlook. Every extended movement is planned in advance and controlled throughout by the shrewdest financial generals in the world. They know the actual—not the published—conditions of the properties whose stocks are to be handled. They know when natural conditions warrant a bull or a bear campaign. They leave nothing to chance, but their trump card is the weakness of human nature.

When the plans have been arranged for a bull campaign, or extended upward movement, every sort of bear argument imaginable is used to induce the public to sell; elections, war scares, stringent money, damaged crops, gold exports, etc., etc., are resurrected and used effectively year after year. Meanwhile, the insiders are quietly accumulating stocks and checking every advance at certain figures. Finally, when all is ready, and the vast majority of speculators bearish and declines seem inevitable, the bull market commences—often upon the actual happening of some anticipated bad news. The advance is at first very gradual; some stocks rise, others remain stationary, while a break is made in one or two, to encourage the bears in putting out more "short lines." Presently the "leaders" advance more rapidly, and the others begin to move up. Each stock has its individual range and peculiarity in moving, though toward the end of a campaign those stocks which have been lagging behind come forward with a rush. The importance, therefore, of confining your attention to the leaders during the first half of a campaign, can readily be seen. The money made on them can be transferred to the "specialties" before the latter have had their advance.

During all this time there have been thousands of fluctuations, like surface waves, but the tide is on the flood and prices steadily rise. Every one becomes enthusiastic over improving business. The "sneaking" bull market has developed into a "creeping" bull market and the "lambs" are at last making money. Finally there comes a grand rush to buy, accompanied with great excitement and the wildest optimistic rumors. Enormous quantities of stocks are handled, and this is the finish, for a time, at least, of the bull campaign. Insiders are "unloading"; and although newspapers, financial writers, news bureaus, and every bull artifice that can be devised, are used to "jolly" the public into buying, though everything looks rosy and there is not a cloud in the financial horizon, the market comes to a stand. Spite of good news prices sag. Gradually but surely and with many false upward starts, the market falls.

Once the insiders have distributed their stocks, absolutely nothing can keep prices up. Before long, excuses are found to force down the market; and then the same old game is played over again. It all resolves itself into two grand divisions: Accumulation—or buncoing marginal and investment owners out of their stocks at less than actual value; and Distribution—or selling the same stocks, by means of false pretenses, at vastly more than actual value.

The details are changed, but the same general tactics are employed year after year. The lambs never learn to buy stocks when everything looks darkest. They never learn that a bull campaign begins in gloom and ends in glory.

POOL METHODS.

Human nature is such that it is almost impossible to buy stocks at the bottom, with nothing but bad news-pouring in. It is still harder to sell at the top when the market looks strong and only goods news is heard, and personal friends tell you of some insider who has assured them of a 15 or 20

169

points advance in such and such a stock. People generally buy at these times. The manipulators' game is to play on this phase of human nature, and they pull the wires so as to get everybody full of financial optimism just at the time when they are ready to sell. Surely anyone can see that the big fellows are not here for their health, or for glory, but to make money, and the largest amount possible, with absolute disregard of whose pocket it comes out of. SOMEBODY must lose the money which they make. See to it that YOU are not one of those somebodies.

In accumulating stocks preparatory to a bull campaign, the usual pool method is to depress prices as far as possible with a view of catching stop orders, etc., then to quickly buy without bidding up prices until the market has advanced three or four points, then work it down again as far as circumstances will permit. After some weeks of feverishness and narrow fluctuations, during which time the pools are quietly gathering in all the stock possible without bidding up prices, the market is allowed to run up five to ten points, and the pools take profits on a portion of their holdings, as a kind of feeler. Then prices are worked down about half the advance, and their sales repurchased. The nest advance may carry the market up ten or fifteen points, and so on. There may be a dozen pools at work all this time in different stocks, but they are all playing the game on practically the same lines.

Before the upward move is fairly under way, and sometimes after the move starts, sudden breaks will be made in a stock to shake out "company" and induce short selling; for if outside traders can be made to think the stock is a sale whenever it "puts its head up," a large and weak short interest can be fostered, which makes upward manipulation easy. A common method, not only by the pools, but by many professional operators, is to divide their holdings into three equal lots; holding one lot perhaps two or three years, for the extreme movement of say 80 points. The second lot is sold at the culmination of each minor bull campaign, perhaps in three or four months, at a profit of twenty to thirty points, and bought back on a reasonable decline. Profits of five to ten points are taken on the third lot, which is also bought back in due course. This method, with but slight variations, was employed by the insiders from August, 1896, to March, 1899. Some operators divide their purchases into four lots instead of three, using the fourth lot entirely for scalping purposes.

When the larger pools are preparing for a bear campaign, they usually begin by holding the market strong, and if possible advance two or three showy, attractive stocks with great ostentation, to fool the public with stories of "Vanderbilt buying," "Standard Oil buying," etc., while they sell the general list at the highest possible prices. The smaller pools, however, and individual professional bears, often cover with as little loss as they can if their short selling and manipulation fail to bring about a decline; and then they help to bid up stocks a few points to where they can again commence selling, and so on until finally a break is forced. Whether the pool be big or little, when at last the market commences going in their favor, they hammer it on the way down, and as the decline continues, liquidation of long stocks is induced, and outside short sellers invariably come in about the time bottom is reached.

Almost every important play which the pools make in stocks is in anticipation of some event. Often the movement culminates just after, and occasionally just before, the happening of this event. When, however, there is a strong element of uncertainty, and even the insiders themselves are not sure of the result, then the movement will probably continue after the anticipation becomes an accomplished fact.

HINTS ON HOW TO WIN.

"In all the stupendous works of nature there is nothing more sublime than the egotism of the man who expects to win when he plays at a game of skill which he does not understand, and has for an opponent an expert who uses marked cards."

But a study of the following facts and suggestions should enable you to play this game with at least a chance of success.

1st.—When a dull, weak market has become active and declining, then panicky, and enormous quantities of stock are changing hands, prices are most likely very near the bottom, and a rally of several points may be expected. After this rally, there is usually a second downward movement to about the previous low figures touched before; but this is not invariable. Stocks bought at such times should be held for good advances, provided other signs indicate that it is the end and not the beginning of a bear campaign.

2d.—If after a dull, sagging market, when everybody is bearish, or after a decline, there comes a rally of 3 or 4 points, and then certain stocks lose ½ to ¾ of this rally, after which they rally again, and this time lose only about half of the latter rally, the next upward move of about a point makes it certain that insiders or pools are accumulating those stocks, which will indicate higher prices. The same movements reversed, when market is at top, indicate lower prices.

3d.—If, after a pronounced general advance, there comes a day of large transactions, excitement and enthusiasm, the advance will suddenly stop and the market react, even if it goes higher ultimately. Then will ensue a period of

2 to 5 points fluctuations, that is, a "traders' market"—just the thing for the "scale" and "fluctuation" systems.

4th.—Keep accurate charts and records of the most active stocks, and endeavor through them to learn what the insiders are doing. When your charts show a great many fluctuations over a narrow range in a certain stock after a decline, and finally the stock advancing beyond this range on heavy transactions, it will be a fair assumption that the insiders or pools have been accumulating that security and intend advancing the price. If your records show that several leading stocks are acting in a similar manner, it is very good evidence that a bull market is ahead.

5th.—After the market has been dragging along a low level for some weeks, with only small fluctuations in prices, then a day or two of extreme dullness, it is safe betting that a bull campaign will soon be under way. When the bears get tired of selling and there are no more stocks offered, the market of course comes to a standstill, and the insiders conclude the time has arrived to advance prices.

6th.—When everything appears to favor lower levels and everybody is bearish, when every possible reason is given why you should sell, when continued bad news comes in—and yet stocks still fluctuate over a narrow range, without going materially lower in spite of short selling by chronic bears—you may be sure the insiders are accumulating, and the next pronounced move should be upward.

7th.—The volume of transactions is an excellent indicator as to the general trend of prices. When the largest volumes are on the advances and trading falls off on the reactions, you can be pretty sure it is a bull market.

8th.—It is usually dangerous to buy stocks on the third day of an advance. The market generally moves two or three days in one direction and then either rests or reacts. If stocks close at top after a three days' advance and open strong next morning, four times out of five they will react a point at least. But if after a three days' rise the market halts, and there is no decided movement either way for a couple of days, the reaction is not likely to occur. The advance will probably be resumed on the third day of this resting period; vice versa after a three days' decline.

9th.—A three days' rampant advance after a prolonged bull market, coupled with enormous transactions, great excitement and enthusiasm—especially on the culmination of expected good news—is an infallible indication that the campaign is over, for a time at least.

10th.—When a stock advances for three days, and on the third day of the advance the total transactions in that stock foot up an enormous total, the move is very likely over. But when, after a period of dullness, a stock begins to advance on heavy transactions, buy it for a three days' rise.

11th.—There are only two ways to trade—either take small losses, or else never take a loss at all. This is a very old rule, but a good one. If a stock goes against you, limit your loss at from half a point to 2 points; especially so in the case of "tips." Or else buy on scale down, first taking very good care to find out that the shares you propose buying are intrinsically worth the current market price. Unless you deal in small lots, or are a capitalist, the limited loss plan is preferable. Another old rule and a good one, is to buy when everybody wants to sell, and sell when everybody is clamoring to buy.

A FEW DONT'S.

DON'T "go short for a turn" in a bull market, or "long" in a bear market, no matter how certain you may be that a reaction is due. It is poor policy to run the risk of losing ten points to scalp one. If you have good profits and expect a reaction, close out if you choose, and buy back cheaper—but DON'T "go short." DON'T shut your eyes to the bear elements in the situation because you are long of stocks. And DON'T be a "chronic bear," blind to all signs of higher prices. DON'T allow your desires and hopes to obscure your judgment; the wish should not be father to the thought. Keep posted on all the elements in the situation and how they are likely to influence public sentiment, but DON'T forget that this is of less importance than a knowledge of how the insiders are working. DON'T be a bull when the public have the stocks, and DON'T be a bear when the floating supply of securities is held by insiders.

DON'T attach importance to the weekly "Bank Statements" or to London quotations; they are often "doctored," and are usually misleading. DON'T read the gossip or "news" in financial papers, brokers' letters, etc. Insiders manipulate the press as they do values, and very little goes into public print that they want to keep out. Don't live over the ticker, unless you are an expert at tape reading; it will only mislead you; nor will you learn anything from the old "rounders" and "tapeworms" who study it. DON'T handle stocks not easily traded in; and DON'T try to get the last fraction when you already have good profits. DON'T fight the course of the market, rather follow it; but if you have been bearish in a bull campaign, DON'T reverse your position and become a bull when the advance is over; If you have been bullish when prices were falling, DON'T become a bear when the bull campaign is about to begin. "Run quickly or not at all." DON'T trade in one stock exclusively, as something might happen; divide your trades over 5 or 6 sound stocks. DON'T over-trade, or carry a larger number of shares than your capital justifies. And DON'T buy on bulges nor sell on breaks.

SYSTEMS.

The two following systems, or rather methods, are as good as any: Use the first toward the end of either a bull or bear campaign, and continue until an extended movement is indicated; then switch over to the second.

Catching the Fluctuations.—During a "traders' market," or a market without any pronounced trend one way or the other, any active stock will move over certain points dozens of times. The plan is to place a note that will catch these daily fluctuations. Buy 100 shares of, say, St. Paul, at the market price, and 100 more every half point up or down, but don't hold more than 100 at a time at the same figure, and don't accumulate more than 600 shares altogether. Treat every purchase as a separate transaction, and whenever a profit of one point net is shown, sell that 100 shares, buying back on a one point reaction. When a purchase and sale are both indicated at the same figure, do nothing—simply hold that 100 shares, but for convenience assume that 100 has been sold and 100 bought. If St. Paul should keep on going up without a reaction, you would thus always be long of 200 shares. Don't get frightened because of a temporary downward tendency. The fluctuations are what bring you profit. Great care must, of course, be taken not to work this system on the bull side if the general trend is downward, or on the bear side if the trend is upward.

Limited Pyramiding.—When the rules and indications already given show that a pronounced upward movement is not far off, buy on weak spots such quantities as your means justify. Do nothing more until the bull campaign gets under way. Then buy small lots with your profits on recessions of half a point, and as much more every half point down. Such recessions are continuous, two or three a day, even in the strongest bull market. Continue these tactics until there come two or three days of rapidly advancing prices, general enthusiasm, and heavy volume of transactions; in other words, when the public are rushing in to buy, and the pools are feeding out some of their stock. Then sell about half your holdings; wait for a reaction of at least a point, and begin buying back every half point down. When the upward movement is resumed follow same plan as before, until the signs and principles laid down in preceding pages show the whole bull market as about to culminate. Then sell out everything on the "bulge." Wait for the third day of a reaction and buy moderately for the "second top." When you get out this time, either take a rest, or return to the "Fluctuation System," playing it on the short side.

FURTHER REMARKS ON
HOW TO PLAY THE GAME SUCCESSFULLY.

Though the same general tactics are pursued year after year, insiders constantly scheme out new tricks to deceive their opponents. If you propose, therefore, to win money instead of losing it, you must not only master the ordinary complications of the game, but also keep up to date, the same as in any other business. Good Judgment, both of conditions and men, is necessary. If you keep charts, keep them properly, and learn how to read them. Do you think a farmer who had never seen the ocean before, could navigate a ship by means of charts? I believe in charts only when other indications point the same way. Watch the volumes of daily transactions. Both bull and bear campaigns culminate in large volumes. By large volumes I mean large as compared with the preceding daily volumes. Don't mistake for this, those times when, after a long period of dullness, certain stocks begin to advance on heavy buying. Time and seasons are to be considered. Four months is the usual length of time for a bull campaign. As a rule, there is also a minor bull campaign in mid-winter. The position on the market of the public and small traders is of great importance. No bull campaign ever started with the public long of stocks, and no bull campaign ever yet ended with the public short. Rates at which stocks are carried on the Exchanges give a clue to the public's position; but as loaning rates on stocks are easily manipulated a better way is to find out from bucket shops or brokerage houses which side their customers are on. If outsiders are all selling, it is pretty safe for you to buy, and vice versa.

When heavy volumes begin to come out the old trader knows there is "something doing." There are times when it is comparatively easy to discern whether activity in a stock will be followed by an advance or a decline. Don't try to trade every day, and don't chase fractions. Unless playing some good scale system, take a quick loss if a purchase or sale goes against you, and start over again. If it goes in your favor, try to get 5 to 20 points, according to what the stock is. One trade closed at a profit of 10 points will more than make up for five losing trades of one point each. As to the usual scale system (that is, buying small lots every point or half point down, and taking profits of one point net on any separate lot). It is all right; but you must first be sure that the stock you propose buying is worth approximately its current market price; then you must put up such big margins in order to be absolutely safe, that your percentage of profit on the investment will usually look very small.

CHAPTER XXXV.

WALL STREET POINTS OF VIEW.

A collection of Wall Street aphorisms, maxims, truisms, proverbs, opinions and points of view, follows:

Hear-say is half lies.
Talk little and well.
Control your temper.
Enough is great riches.
No one is always right.
The first loss is the best.
All players cannot win.
Press luck to the finish.
There is luck in leisure.
Cheap advice is plentiful.
A true word needs no oath.
Done leisurely—done well.
Negotiate before slaughter.
When in doubt do nothing.
After one loss comes many.
Wall Street easily forgets.
Great vaunters, little doers.
Learn to take a loss quickly.
Information makes a market.
Nothing risked, nothing won.
For a lost thing care nothing.

Losses make us more cautious.
Little and often fills the purse.
All is not lost that is in peril.
When wisdom fails, luck helps.
Punctual pay gets willing loan.
Let profits run; limit all losses.
Some men learn only by failing.
Losers are always in the wrong.
Cut a loss and let a profit run.
A thing well bought is half sold.
A plunger gets but seldom holds.
Interrogate before you negotiate.
Money is most valued when lost.
Everyone is wise after the event.
At a great bargain make a pause.
Don't buy an egg until it is laid.
Under fair words beware of fraud.
Liberal hands make many friends.
Novelty always appears handsome.
Business neglected is business lost.
After extreme weakness buy stocks.
More sheep than lambs are sheared.
Better lose the wool than the sheep.
It is fortune, not wisdom that rules.
Fraud is built on misrepresentation.
Don't put all your eggs in one basket.
Better lose the saddle than the horse.
The market will be here to-morrow.
Small losses often prove great gains.
Men often seem rich to become rich.
Inspiration often means perspiration

By the husk you may guess at the nut.
Hear the other side and believe little.
Beware of one who has nothing to lose.
Speculation begins when certainty ends.
The rich buy in a hurry when they buy.
In a traders' market buy low—sell high.
Delay overmuch is oftentimes great risk.
An old man's sayings are seldom untrue.
Get an investment that will let you sleep.
They who lose to-day may win to-morrow.
Opportunity is often lost by deliberating.
Illusions ruin all those whom they blind.
The maxims of men disclose their hearts.
The poorer the sheep, the harder it bleats.
A little loss frightens—a great one tames.
Where something is found there look again.
He that will have eggs must have cackling.
The best is always the cheapest in the end.
Liberality is not giving largely, but wisely.
Get information before you invest, not after.
Thrice happy they who have an occupation.
Wisdom adorns riches, and shadows poverty.
No lock will hold against the power of gold.
Begin to buy when prices are dull and weak.
Satisfy the rich and they will pay your price.
He is a wise man who wears poverty decently.
Great minds have purposes; others have wishes.
An ounce of luck is worth a pound of wisdom.
Great undertakings require great preparations.
Of what use is a 10 per cent margin in a panic?
The rich man does not know who is his friend.

A man gets no thanks for what he loses at play.

They who live in a worry invite death in a hurry.

Soft words and hard arguments catch the investor.

Put your eggs in one basket and watch the basket.

Every time the sheep bleats it loseth a mouthful.

The rich are meanest when they buy small things.

The rich man is apt to be more generous than just.

He swears who is accustomed to his own false words.

Money easily made, easily goes; easy come, easy go.

If you do not hear reason, she will rap your knuckles.

He who prates of his wisdom doth but conceal an ass.

Provide for the worst; the best will take care of itself.

It is an old maxim that accidents usually help the bears.

Lend money without bond and you but make an enemy.

The advice of successful men only is worth application.

A man with long hair is generally rash and impetuous.

A man must make his opportunity as often as he finds it.

Things in motion sooner catch the eye than what not stirs.

He who sells what isn't his'n, must buy it back or go
to pris'n.

Sell and borrow only those stocks which have a
wide market.

Some had rather guess at much than take pains to
learn a little.

Men of wit and facts never need be driven to
indirect courses.

To estimate a man's wealth, divide the gossip estimates
by four.

To grasp an opportunity with firm decision marks an
able man.

After advancing markets, and prices waver, lower prices
will come.

When prices are high, or there is a declining tendency, sell on rallies.

Much money made before twenty is apt to be lost in the reign of plenty.

He is rich enough who has no debts, and young enough who has health.

"Early information" and a big bank account will be the ruin of any man.

Moderate riches will carry you; if you have more, you must carry them.

The success of a manipulated market depends largely on sustained activity.

It is idle to wait for your ship to come in unless you have sent one out.

When prices close weak without support, a rally will be in order next morning.

He who takes no care of little things will not have the care of great ones.

When prices are low, or there is an advancing tendency, buy on fair concessions.

A lordly taste makes a beggar's purse; a champagne appetite but a purse for beer.

A wise leader watches closely the current of events and goes with it—not against it.

Learn which side of the market he is on and you quickly discover the cause of the pain.

When prices close strong, after an all-day advance, the next move is generally downward.

Judgment is the best protector of energy; information is the best protector for resources.

Those who lament their misfortunes are generally they who do not recognize their opportunities.

He who loses money loses much; he who loses a friend loses more, but he who loses his spirit loses all.

If the trade goes in your favor, follow it until the last trade goes against you, then close the transaction.

When there is much excitement and high prices for everything, the market should be sold for a good turn.

He that at twenty understands nothing, at thirty knows nothing, at forty has nothing, will lead a wretched old age.

It seems to be a law of panics that the stocks which have the largest preceding advances have also the largest declines.

When you buy and the trade goes in your favor, follow it up; but when the last purchase goes against you, close the transaction and take your profits on all the other trades.

A market which halts after a rise, which becomes irregular and which develops weak spots, is more apt to foster falling than rising prices, although this is not invariably the case.

In active markets, an advancing or declining movement will generally run three or four days, when it becomes exhausted, and an opportunity is offered for making a profitable turn in the opposite direction.

"Believing a stock had reached the top of an advance, I sold it short five times losing each time before I caught the swing. My losses were speedily recovered and I closed out with a handsome profit on the deal."—A Successful Trader.

A halt in a bull period almost always starts with something which lessens confidence in credits. When credits begin to shrink, business begins to contract, and as this throws labor out of employment, the great circle is established and generally runs until self-correction takes place. It is one of the Street theories that a triple-top followed by relapse is evidence of coming large decline. This, however, is not sufficiently certain to justify action except when supported by substantial reasons. It does suggest, however, that the forces which tend to check advance become strong about that level.

In a relapse, after a large advance, there are usually two stages; first, a quick decline, due to bear attacks and the execution of stop orders, and second, a slow fall on the preponderance of selling over buying orders. The decline is often very irregular, full of rallies and making, as seen from day to day, a feverish trading market.

It should always be remembered that credit falls as rapidly as it rises and that it is possible for credit resources to be swept away not only by decreases in actual values, but by any loss of confidence which restricts operations on a large scale. Credit is and must remain the basis of business, the basis of speculation, and the foundation on which values rest.

When the market stops going up and momentum is lost, there usually grows up a balance of selling, which gradually brings declines. At such time, it is always wise to endeavor to sell when the market is very strong and not when it is weak, as rallies always frighten bears at the top of an advance, just as a bull is always weakest in his stomach at the time when he ought to have most strength.

All systems at times work out well. Most or all of them break down in practice sooner or later, partly, however, through the inability or unwillingness of traders to follow them when following the rule becomes expensive or dangerous. Many systems are founded upon the tendency in the market toward action and reaction, and they are oftentimes a help, but should always be put in a secondary place, the preference being given to values.

Buyers of stocks belong to two classes: those who trade on tendencies and who take hold wherever the market is active without much reference to values or prices, and those who always try to buy when prices are off instead of when they are up. A powerful interest undertaking to handle the market will try to get both classes of buyers; hence will resist the market at times to encourage one set and permit reactions at another to encourage others.

All stocks will move more or less with the general market, but value will tell in the long run. The policy of buying the best stocks on declines is almost always justified by the event. The policy of selling the worst stocks on advances is theoretically wise, but is sometimes upset in practice, because so many people do the same thing as to keep the stock strong by the covering that takes place, but in this case, also, value will finally determine the price.

Manipulation of stocks, as it is termed in Wall Street, is a process that has for its object the forcing or the persuading of other people to buy or sell a given stock or bond. Where force is used once, persuasion is probably used twenty times. It is difficult to force anyone to buy something at a given price unless he feels that he must have it. It is often a relatively easy task to induce people to buy something by making them think that they want it.

Cycles in business may not be subject to scientific demonstration, but the theory has for a century worked well in practice. The reasons given why business should increase for a number of years, and then for a number of years run backwards may or may not be sound. But action based on belief that this will occur has been sound. When the turn comes, there is always something to help the movement along, no matter whether the tendency is up or down.

A lesson taught by panics is that in times of great fear and anxiety values are disregarded and the best stocks go off as much or more than the worst. Indeed, when people have to have money they sell the best stocks because there is some market for them, while there is no market at all for others. Furthermore, the best stocks are likely to be in loans and loans are sold out while the poorer stocks, which have been paid for, do not come out because they are not forced out.

It must be remembered that when large operators have committed themselves on one side or the other, they cannot change their position quickly, as can be done by smaller traders. They are oftentimes obliged to stick to a position for awhile, even when they would be glad to change. It is equally true and equally important to remember that large operators must disregard temporary conditions, and they make their money by persistence and by overcoming difficulties.

There is no way of telling when the top of an advance or the bottom of a decline has been reached until some time after such top or bottom has been made. Sometimes people are able to guess when prices are at the top or at the bottom, but such guessers are of their nature of no particular value, and it is a proverb in Wall Street that only a foolish speculator hopes to buy stocks at the lowest and sell them at the highest. The speculator with experience knows that no one can do this with certainty or regularity.

"There is never any news on a bull market. The only time when news in its fullest sense is effective is when receiverships, bankruptcies and disasters generally are pending. Then the news is effective in forcing breaks. Now the idea prevails as always that no news is good news. There are times when the market is helped by news, as in a time of panic, when some statement is made of forthcoming steps by banking interests to protect the market. Such action causes a rally after a break or acts as a check to forced legislation."—Peter Bennett.

Whenever the market moves out of a narrow rut, stop orders are essential. While the market remains within narrow limits stop orders are a needless waste of money. There is no way of telling when the market will change from narrow swings to a prolonged move except by a steady watch of what takes place. If, as a result of days of trading there is increasing weakness, the chances are for decline. If the market hardens on trading, the chances are for advance. As long as strength and weakness seem to about balance each other, the chances are for short turns.

When large operators enter upon a stock campaign, the first thing they do is to provide funds on a scale commensurate with the undertaking. They either borrow or arrange to borrow great sums of money. This money, or its credit equivalent, is loaned by a bank to an individual, but when deposited by the individual it becomes a deposit of the bank. This is why loans and deposits usually move together. What the banks give out as loans they take in as deposits. Hence, a large expansion in loans and deposits means that some interest has borrowed a great deal of money and is either using it on account of some past transactions, or is holding it for some future use.

The movement of the market is always in swings. The center point stands for close approximation to values.

Where prices go down, the momentum carries them too far and when they go up the same thing occurs; hence reaction in both is inevitable. The same thing is true with regard to small speculative movements. If the price of a stock is run up two or three points, it very generally swings back about half of the amount of the advance. There are exceptions where changes in value or a fixed speculative purpose makes an abnormal movement, but in a free-trading stock there is more than an average chance that any primary movement will be followed by a reacting movement of at least three-eighths of the first swing.

Panics in the stock market have a well defined course. The record since 1873 shows only two exceptions to the rule, the rule prevailing in all other cases. A panicky market usually lasts during parts of three days, although this is not invariable. The lowest prices are usually made on the second day. From those prices there is a recovery amounting usually to more than half the amount of the decline from the level of prices prevailing before the panic. This recovery culminates within a week and sometimes not for thirty days, but in all cases prior to the May 9, 1901 panic, within thirty days. After that comes a slow decline during which prices lose at least half of their recovery and in case of a bear market all the recovery and more is lost.

Nothing is more common than to hear people say that the big bankers can do what they please with the stock market, and yet nothing is further from the truth. The stock market is in the end made by the public and by no one else, if the smaller fluctuations and minor "swings" be disregarded. Traders can move prices within narrow limits; bankers can move them within wider limits, but without the public the market tends constantly to equilibrium. Stocks go off when traders sell and rally when they cover; stocks advance when bankers bid them up, but decline unless the public buys on the advance. Both traders and bankers can and generally do anticipate the public in its operations, but if the public does not do what is expected of it nothing is gained thereby.

The investor determines the prices of stocks in the long run. This statement is sometimes disputed by those who point to the fluctuations which are confessedly made by manipulators without regard to value. It is true that such fluctuations occur, but when the manipulation is over the voice of the investor is again heard. If he decides that a given stock is worth only so much, the manipulator will ultimately be compelled to accept that valuation because manipulation cannot be kept up. The object of manipulation is to buy below value and sell above value. The experience of all traders will afford many illustrations of how stocks have recovered after artificial depression and relapsed after artificial advances to the middle point which represented value as it was understood by those who bought or held as investors.

The evident uncovering of many stop-loss orders on a decline moved an old trader to belittle their use for speculative protection. "When a man," said he, "gives his broker a stop order he thinks that only he and his broker know it. But the broker, being a busy man, turns the stop over to some two-dollar specialist in that particular stock. In the course of a week, or two weeks, the principal specialists in any active stock accumulate a large number of such orders. Then the manipulating interests go to them and say: 'What have you got in the way of stops?' The specialists disclose what they have, and if the stops are abundant enough the manipulating interests say: 'Shake them out.' That's why it so often happens that a stock moves just far enough against you to catch your stop and then moves back again."

Daily fluctuations in the stock market are influenced by sentiment. There are perhaps 400 men who trade more or less on the floor of the Exchange. They are not generally the class of operators who try to forecast the somewhat distant future, but their object in their daily trading is to act promptly on such news and developments as come to them hour by hour. Practice in this has made the professional traders extremely skillful in detecting signs of changes in the market and in reading anything that is likely to affect trading. The result is that the attention of these operators is apt to be fixed on one or two prominent facts and the trading of all hinges more or less on developments at those points. If the market is declining and it begins to rally on some special news or special buying, traders all want to buy at the same time, causing the speed of the recovery. Or, if news is unfavorable, the room wants to sell all at the same time, causing the rapidity and the extent of decline.

Value has little to do with temporary fluctuations in stock prices, but is the determining factor in the long run. Values, when applied to stocks, are determined, in the end, by the return to the investor, and nothing is more certain than that the investor establishes the price of stocks. The manipulator is all-powerful for a time. He can mark prices up or down. He can mislead investors, inducing them to buy when he wishes to sell, and to sell, when he wishes to buy; but manipulation in a stock cannot be permanent, and in the end the investor learns the approximate truth. His decision to keep his stock or to sell it then makes a price independent of speculation and, in a large sense, indicative of true value. It is so indicative because the price made is well known to insiders, who also know better than anyone else the true value of the stock. If the price is too low, insiders will buy; hence stability in the price of a stock means that insiders do not think the stock especially cheap or dear.

Early information affecting stock market fluctuations is dangerous to trifle with and the story of the "Minister and the Stock Exchange," as told in the following letter to the *London Spectator,* illustrates the point:

Sir: Permit me to impart to you the substance of a family legend. My grandfather was a city man, a Member of Parliament, and an adherent of the Grenville party. On matters connected with "the city" the politician was in the habit of consulting the city man in question. On one occasion when the subject of conversation was the possibility of realizing large profits from early information, Lord Grenville asked my grandfather whether he thought all the stories told of these large profits were founded on fact. My grandfather answered that he was not a stockjobber, still less a political authority, but that he could easily test the matter if Lord Grenville wished it. His Lordship then said: "I will give you the earliest information obtainable in the position I hold as Prime Minister, and you shall try your fortune and mine in dealing on the Stock Exchange."

At the end of a year the statesman and merchant met again to study the account after the earliest information given by the Prime Minister to the city man had been acted on. My grandfather rendered the account, and showed that, had the information led to transactions on a large scale, all parties connected with them would have been utterly ruined.

When the battle of Waterloo was fought it was not the Government which told the news to Rothschild, but Rothschild who told it to the Government.

In my own experience I have known the man with the most brilliant prospects granted to any one utterly disgraced and ruined by attempting to deal in the manner suggested. His own description of what occurred will suffice. He had not a minute's peace all the morning till the evening paper came in with the news obtained by its editor, not by the speculator's exclusive information.

H. R. G.

If the public would realize one thing, and realize it so that it never forgot it, its chances in Wall Street would be materially improved. From the Wall Street point of view—meaning thereby the sentiment prevailing as a whole, and on an average on the part of the speculative and financial community—the public has money which Wall Street desires that it shall exchange for securities. It is true that so far as a large section of the Street is concerned there is not the slightest desire to knowingly sell worthless securities to the public. The essence, however, of the matter is that Wall Street is always in the position of selling securities to the public for money, sometimes being able to sell easily and in quantity, and at other times not being able to sell much, and that only with difficulty. The public should remember that all the manipulation of Wall Street has but one end, namely, to exchange securities for money. For in the long run the public does not sell securities. What it buys and pays for it generally keeps. Once stocks have been sold to the public they seldom or never return in any quantity to the Street.

Jay Gould said once that the first requisite for successful speculation was patience. Most operators realize that they have cut short their profits, frequently and needlessly, by the lack of patience. A great movement in the market does not usually come suddenly. The market, while manipulated in a narrow sense, is in its large sense created by conditions. The prices of stocks act as a sort of skirmish line, out in front of the developments that have actually occurred, and in the direction of those which are expected to occur. When they get too far out, they have to fall back. Then, when the facts become clear, they move for a time with a rush. When the tide is nearly in or nearly out, there is a period of slack water. When the business tide is nearly in or nearly out, there is a period when it is impossible to say definitely that conditions have changed in a large way either for better or for worse. Some conditions may have changed and others not, with the balance doubtful. This makes a corresponding situation in the stock market. Prices go off on that which is unfavorable and recover again on that which is favorable. The net change during such a time may be small even if the market is fairly active and the gross changes are quite large.

"Addison Cammack, a great bear trader in his day, believed in Napoleon's famous dictum: 'The Lord is on the side of the heaviest battalions.' That is, he would start to sell the market; if it yielded, he would follow up the advantage with an avalanche of selling orders; he overwhelmed his opponents. The simple question was could he sell more stock than the other side was able to or willing to buy. If the heavier battalion happened to be on the other side and the market continued to advance he quickly beat a retreat so as to be able to fight another day. And this is the difference between the big, wise bear and the foolish little bear. The big bear knows that some time conditions will be ripe to hammer the market. He tries it occasionally. Frequently he makes a mistake, but he withdraws from the field with his resources practically intact. His opportunity surely comes, and then there is dismay among the bulls. The cub specimen, however, does not know enough to run away from danger. He continues to fight when there is no fighting chance. That is why Addison Cammack retired from the field with the reputation of having been a very big and dangerous bear, while so many cubs with bear instincts never grew up into fearsome objects."—Schuyler West.

Question—In answer to an inquiry, you say $1,000 is the proper margin for trading in 10 shares. In most stocks listed $1,000 would more than pay outright for 10 shares. In many stocks listed $1,000 would pay outright for 20 shares. Will you, therefore, be good enough to explain your meaning? Should not the size of the margin be governed by the nature of the security bought, and by the purchase value, rather than by any arbitrary rule?—Z.

Answer—There is a general impression that $1,000 is a fair margin for 100 shares of stock. Perhaps no one idea in speculation has cost traders more money. If a man buys 100 shares, with 10 per cent margin, he is in no position to average his account, and moderate losses absorb his capital so rapidly as to leave him little option except to lose money. The man who looked upon $1,000 as the proper margin for dealing in 10 shares would, as you say, buy outright in some cases. But, supposing his first purchase to have been made on an estimate of value, he would be able to buy a second lot, and even a third lot, if it should become necessary and his opinion of value was unchanged. The ability to stay and to average wisely would mean a profit in the end. The great curse of speculation is overtrading. If operators would work on a basis illustrated by the relation of $1,000 to 10 shares, they would be very much surer of making money than they are now. The amount of margin is not to be considered with reference to the initial purchase, but as bearing upon the ability of the trader to stay in the market and to turn and take advantage of such opportunities as may occur. This cannot be done without a large factor of safety.

"There is always a disposition in people's minds to think that existing conditions will be permanent. When the market is down and dull, it is hard to make people believe that this is the prelude to a period of activity and advance. When prices are up and the country is prosperous, it is always said that while preceding booms have not lasted, there are circumstances connected with this one which make it unlike its predecessors and give assurance of permanency. The one fact pertaining to all conditions is that they will change. This change follows modifications of the law of supply and demand. The cycle of trade is well known. Beginning with a period of depression, the small dealer finds himself unable to buy the amount of goods required for hand-to-mouth trading quite as cheaply as when the previous purchase was made. He, therefore, buys a little more. The aggregate of this buying increases the business of the jobber and this swells the output of the manufacturer, who is enabled to employ more labor, resulting in larger purchases by labor of manufactured goods and agricultural products, which brings the circle round to the producer. At each step in the proceedings, rising prices bring increased purchases and increased confidence, until the retailer buys without hesitation many times the amount of goods which he would have dared to take at the beginning of the cycle of improving trade. This multiplied by millions makes the demand which at times seems inexhaustible, which supplies the railroads with tonnage, and which in its ramifications creates the investment fund which finally seeks employment in Wall Street. The declining period is accompanied by steady reversal of these varied transactions. When the retailer and the jobber find that goods cost less than before they shrink purchases. When purchases in advance of requirements bring loss and not profit, they bring also loss of confidence and curtailment of demand. As the process of shrinkage goes on, it touches all points of trade. It is a kind of flame which creates the fuel which is burned. Experience has shown that it takes about five years for one of these cycles to complete itself. It takes approximately five years for the country bare of stocks to become the country filled with stocks, and it takes about five years more for the over-stocked markets of the country or of the world to become practically bare. As the stock market is always an effect and never a cause, it must respond to these conditions. As, however, the stock market, while an effect, is also a discounted effect, the decline in prices of stocks usually anticipates decline in commodities, because operators for a fall sell in anticipation of the changes which they foresee in business conditions."—Dow.

"It is true in finance as it is in philosophy or in any subject of mortal thought that the general tendency of weak human nature is to believe what one wants to believe rather than what is so. The judgments formed by the great mass of people are apt to be those of idiosyncrasy, passion or temperament, rather than of calm and poised reflection. Few men are so constituted that they can look facts and facts alone in the face and form conclusions uncolored by native optimism or pessimism. A corollary proposition is that few people, as a rule, take pains in their investigation of financial matters or go cautiously from general belief to a specific position. In buying or selling securities it is the vague and glittering that is apt to determine their action rather than the detailed and the substantial. And there is no part of human activity, looked at from the mere worldly point of view, in which just these qualities of accurate and balanced thinking are so necessary as in the financial world. If a man has a bond does he know exactly what is its lien? If he is interested in a company as a stockholder, does he look carefully into the company's annual report and make up his mind accurately as to the wisdom of the dividends paid and the true significance of the various amounts charged for operating expenses and depreciation? An incident which may fairly be called a part of recent financial history, and which should be adverted to because of the lesson it carries of this need of rigorous scrutiny in financial matters, is the story told of those bondholders of the Chicago, Milwaukee and St. Paul Railway who allowed a valuable privilege to lapse because of their ignorance concerning the meaning of the obligation possessed by them. Too late they discovered that they must receive payments upon their bonds at par, when a few weeks before they could have converted the bonds into preferred stock worth nearly double the sum received. Nothing could be plainer than the declaration contained in the bond that the privilege of conversion it offered should be exercised only at a certain time and in a certain way. Yet many of the bondholders were wholly inappreciative of it. Nor is carelessness in such matters confined to people who are untrained in finance. It is trustworthily stated that a great man in one of the banking houses having much to do with the great Northern Pacific fight for control, admitted that not until he had so far engaged in the battle for the possession of the Northern Pacific shares that he could not retreat from it, had he read the certificate of the preferred stock, upon whose disputed construction the question of defeat or victory in the struggle depended. A very much surprised man he was when he found that there were clauses in the certificate of which he was not aware."—Daniel Kellogg (Philip King).

A correspondent writes: I have several points' profit in Atchison and in Missouri Pacific. I cannot see the market more than once a day and I am afraid that my profit will run away before I know it. At the same time I hope for more profit by holding on. What can I do?

The thing to do in this case is to put a stop order in your stock and keep it about two points below the highest price. Missouri Pacific has sold at 117½. Tell your broker to sell if Missouri Pacific falls back to 115½. If Missouri Pacific goes to 118½ raise your stop order to 116½. Keep this up until the stop order is executed or until you are satisfied to take the profit which you have. For an out-of-town operator, no method of trading, once a profit has been established, is any more satisfactory than this. When a bull campaign is fairly under way in a stock, the price frequently advances a greater part of the movement without a reaction of two points. Some operators think 2½ points a little safer, as sometimes a two point stop is just sufficient to spoil a handsome profit. In a large percentage of cases, however, if a stock drops back two points it will drop more than two points. An operator running a bull campaign likes to see reactions of about a point, because they enable him to test the market frequently and to see if the public is following his manipulation. But he does not like to see reactions go much further, because they would have a tendency to chill the bull enthusiasm which he wishes to create. Success, from his standpoint, means a growing public interest which will gradually absorb the stock which he has to sell. This interest can be kept up only by a comparatively large market, a well sustained tone and a gradual rise. Hence, the reason for putting a stop about two points from the highest. The manipulating interest, as long as the campaign lasts, will be certain to have a good volume of buying orders in a stock after it has had about one point decline unless there is some special reason for a change of tactics. Ordinarily a stock which has had a 10 point rise is kept for some time around the upper level of prices. It takes a little time to accumulate stock and a little time to market it, and during the marketing process, the price has to be kept strong and given the appearance of going higher. An operator who wishes to sell 10,000 shares of stock at an advance would usually have to be a large buyer at the higher prices in order to be able to sell. His hope would be that for every thousand shares of stock bought he would be able to sell twelve or fourteen hundred, and that this process would gradually exhaust his line. The follower in a campaign has the advantage that he can sometimes see evidences of this realizing and obtain therefrom a hint as to when it is best for him to sell. If not, the stop order is apt to prove his best friend. He loses two points that he might have made, but by waiting for the stop order to be executed he often makes more than two points which he would not have obtained had he relied upon his judgment as to the best time to sell.

It is an article of faith with many operators that dullness is always followed by decline. The basis for this belief is that during certain periods this occurs, and the repetitions are regarded as establishing a rule. The fact is, however, that the action of the market after dullness depends chiefly upon whether a bull market or a bear market is in progress. In a bull market, dullness is generally followed by advances; in a bear market, by decline. As bear markets as a rule last longer than bull markets, dullness is followed by decline rather oftener than by advance. There are exceptions, but they do not alter the general rule. The reason why in a bull market, dullness is followed by advance, is that a bull market is the exponent of increasing values. Values go on increasing, while the market rests, and prices start up because it becomes apparent to cliques or individuals that values are above prices, and that there is margin for rise. Exactly the reverse argument applies to declines after dullness in a bear period. Prices fall because values are falling, and dullness merely allows the fall in values to get ahead of the fall in prices. The start after a period of inactivity is generally due either to some special event or to manipulation. In the former case, the reason for acting is obvious. In the latter case, manipulators begin by studying the situation and reach a conclusion that it will pay them to move prices. They then scrutinize the speculative situation, and learn something of the position of traders; whether they are carrying a good many stocks or not; whether they seem disposed to deal; whether margins appear to be large or small; and whether specialists have large scale orders to either buy or sell. This gives a basis on which manipulation begins. The public often follows the lead given, sometimes to its own advantage and sometimes to the advantage of the manipulators. All this, however, is merely an incident in the main tendency of prices, which, as a whole, is in accord with the values which grow out of changes in earnings. Temporary movements in the market should always be considered with reference to their bearing on the main movement. The great mistake made by the public is paying attention to prices instead of to values. Whoever knows that the value of a particular stock is rising under conditions which promise stability, and the absence of developments calculated to neutralize the effect of increasing earnings, should buy that stock whenever it declines in sympathy with other stocks, and hold it until the price is considered high enough for the value as it is believed to exist. This implies study and knowledge of the stock chosen, but this marks the difference between intelligent trading and mere gambling. Anybody can guess whether a stock will go up or down, but it is only guessing and the cost of guessing will eat up most of the net profits of trading on pure guesses. Intelligent trading begins with study of conditions, and a justified opinion that the general situation is either growing better or worse. If general conditions are improving, ascertain if the particular stock to be dealt in is having a fair share of that general improvement. Is its value rising? If so, determine whether the price of the stock is low or high with reference to that value. If it is low, buy the stock and wait. Do not be discouraged if it does not move. The more value goes on increasing, the greater the certainty that rise in the stock will come. When it does come, do not take two or three points profit and then wait for a reaction, but consider whether the stock is still cheap at the advance, and if so, buy more, rather than sell under the assumption that the expected rise is underway. Keep the stock until the price appears to be up to the value and get a substantial profit. This is the way the large operators make their money; not by trading back and forth, but by accurate forecasts of coming changes in value, and then buying stocks in quantity and putting the price up to value. The small operator cannot put prices up, but if his premises are sound, he can hold stock with assurance that large operators and investors will put the price up for him.

her Investing Classics available at Traders' Library...

Tape Reading & Market Tactics
by Humphrey B. Neill

1970 edition of the 1931 classic. Neill tells not only how to read the tape, but also how to figure out what's going on behind the numbers. Full of graphs and charts, this book contains excellent sections on human nature and speculation. This is a not-to-be-missed bestseller about the mechanics that drive price action.

ISBN: 978-1-59280-262-3
$13.50

The Art of Speculation by Philip L. Carret

First published in 1930, this legendary perspective shows what affect speculation, or trading as it is commonly referred to today, has on the markets, business, and the onomy this classic has been a mandatory text for any one looking to take money from the markets. Put Carret's in-hts into value investing, market forecasting, and volatility work in your trading today and leverage tactics that have stood the test of time.

ISBN: 978-1-59280-261-6
$13.50

Think and Grow Rich by Napoleon Hill

Since its release in 1937, this book has been an influence on more successful people than almost any other title. Written from research in interviews with the industry giants like Thomas Edison, John D. Rockefeller, Alexander Graham Bell, and many others, this guide breaks the path to success into 13 steps. Find out what these steps are and how they can transform you life.

ISBN: 978-1-59280-260-9
$13.50

WWW.TRADERSLIBRARY.COM